CONNECTED MATHEMATICS® 3

# Additional Practice and Skills Workbook

# Grade 7

**Glenda Lappan**
**Elizabeth Difanis Phillips**
**James T. Fey**
**Susan N. Friel**

**PEARSON**

Connected Mathematics® was developed at Michigan State University with financial support from the Michigan State University Office of the Provost, Computing and Technology, and the College of Natural Science.

 This material is based upon work supported by the National Science Foundation under Grant No. MDR 9150217 and Grant No. ESI 9986372. Opinions expressed are those of the authors and not necessarily those of the Foundation.

As with prior editions of this work, the authors and administration of Michigan State University preserve a tradition of devoting royalties from this publication to support activities sponsored by the MSU Mathematics Enrichment Fund.

13-digit ISBN 978-0-328-90120-3
10-digit ISBN 0-328-90120-2

1 2 3 4 5 6 7 8 9 10   20 19 18 17 16

# Table of Contents

## Additional Practice (continued)

**Draw the polygons described. If there is more than one (or no) shape that you can draw, explain how you know that.**

**5.** Draw a triangle $SRT$. Side $\overline{SR}$ = 3 inches. Side $\overline{RT}$ = 3 inches. $m\angle TRS = 120°$.

**6.** Draw a parallelogram $ABCD$. $m\angle CBA = 75°$ and $m\angle BAD = 40°$.

**7.** Draw a triangle $ABC$. Side $\overline{AB}$ = 12 centimeters. Side $\overline{BC}$ = 6 centimeters. Side $\overline{CA}$ = 20 centimeters.

**8.** Draw an isosceles trapezoid $JKLM$. $m\angle JKL = 60°$ and $m\angle KLM = 120°$. Side $\overline{JK}$ = 2 inches and side $\overline{KL}$ = 2 inches.

# Additional Practice: Digital Assessments

**9.** Jose drew this shape. What is true regarding his shape? *Select all that apply.*

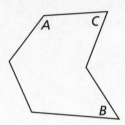

☐ The shape is a polygon.

☐ Angle *A* is acute.

☐ Angle *B* is acute.

☐ Angle *A* is complementary to angle *B*.

☐ Angle *B* is supplementary to angle *C*.

**10.** Determine each angle measure using an angle measuring tool and the values from the bank. Values may be used more than once.

| 95° | 100° | 105° | 110° | 120° |
|-----|------|------|------|------|
| 125° | 130° | 135° | 140° | 180° |

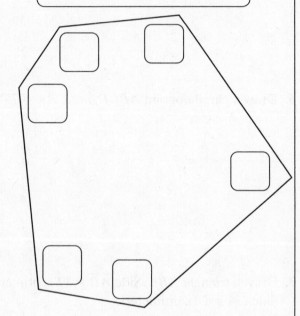

**11.** Write the letter of each angle in the correct box.

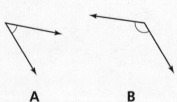   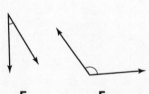

A          B          C          D          E          F

| Acute Angle | Obtuse Angle | Right Angle |
|-------------|--------------|-------------|
|             |              |             |

Name _____ ate _____ Class _____

# Skill: Polygons

**1.** Tell whether each figure is a polygon. Explain how you knov

a.

b.
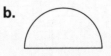

c.
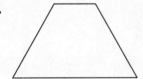

d.
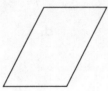

e.

f.

Name _____ Date _____ Class _____

# Skill: Polygons (continued)

2. Tell whether each figure is a polygon. Explain how you know.

a.

b.

c.

d.

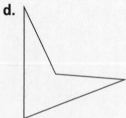

e.

f.

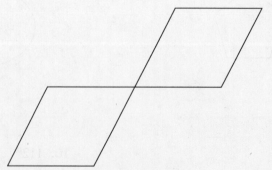

# Skill: Angles

Estimate the measure of each angle. Then check your answer with an angle ruler or a protractor.

**1.**

**2.**

**3.**

**4.**

**5.**

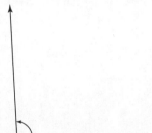

**6.**

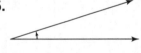

Draw an angle for each measure.

**7.** 165°

**8.** 25°

**9.** 80°

**10.** 112°

# Additional Practice

**Answer parts (a) and (b) for each polygon shown in Exercises 1–6.**

   **a.** Is the shape a regular polygon? Explain why or why not.


   **b.** Could the shape be used to tile a surface? Make a sketch to demonstrate
        your answer.

**1.**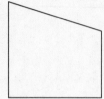

**2.**

**3.**

**4.**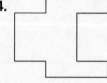

**5.**

**6.**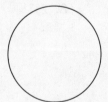

# Additional Practice (continued)

7. The shape below is composed of four polygons.

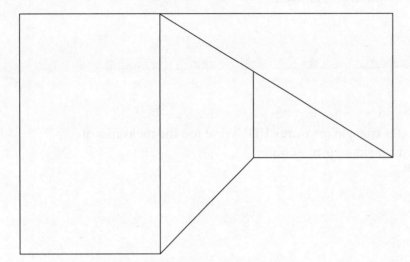

   **a.** Describe the four polygons in the shape.

   **b.** Can the shape be used to tile a surface? Make a sketch to demonstrate
      your answer.

# Additional Practice (continued)

8. An isosceles triangle has two 50° angles. What is the measure of the third angle? Explain how you found your answer.

9. One angle of an isosceles triangle measures 100°. What are the measures of the other two angles? Explain your reasoning.

10. Two of the angles of a parallelogram each measure 75°. What are the measures of the other two angles? Explain your reasoning.

11. One angle of a parallelogram measures 40° and another angle measures 140°. What are the measures of the other two angles? Explain how you found your answer.

# Additional Practice *(continued)*

**12.** Can a parallelogram have two 45° angles and two 75° angles? Why or why not?

**13.** For each of the shapes below, find the unknown angle measure without using your angle ruler.

**a.**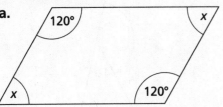

**b.**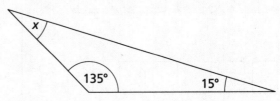

**c.**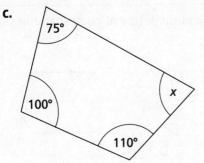

**d.**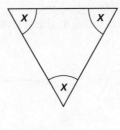

# Additional Practice: Digital Assessments

**14.** An isosceles triangle has two angles measuring 40°. Use the tiles below to write an equation to find the measure of the third angle.

| 40 | 50 | 180 | 360 |

| + | − | × | ÷ |

☐ ☐ ☐ ☐ ☐ = ☐

**15.** Use values from the bank to label the missing angle measures.

| 48° 77° 103° 107° 119° 128° 138° |

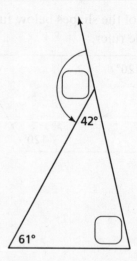

42°

61°

**16.** Which of these objects can be used to tile a surface? Write the letter of each shape in the correct box.

  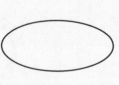  

A        B        C        D        E

| **Can Tile a Surface** |
|---|
|  |

| **Cannot Tile a Surface** |
|---|
|  |

# Skill: Angle Sums and Exterior Angles of Polygons

**Find the measure of each angle labeled x.**

**1.**

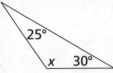

**2.**

**3.**

**4.**

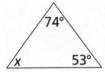

**5.**

**6.**

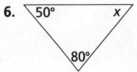

**Find the measure of each angle labeled x.**

**7.**

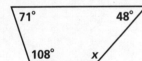

**8.**

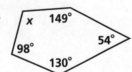

**9.**

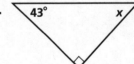

Name _____ Date _____ Class _____

# Skill: Angle Sums and Exterior Angles of Polygons

**Find the measure of angle 1 in each figure.**

10.

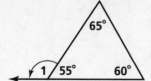

11.

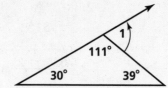

12.

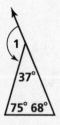

13.

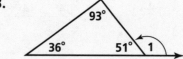

14.

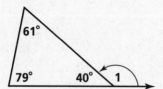

15.

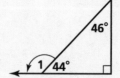

# Additional Practice

1. A quadrilateral has two sides of length 6. The sum of the lengths of the other two sides is 15. Use this information to answer the following questions.

   **a.** Suppose the two sides of length 6 are right next to each other. What might the lengths of the other two sides be? Explain your reasoning.

   **b.** Suppose the quadrilateral is a rectangle and the two sides of length 6 are opposite each other. What would the lengths of the other two sides have to be? Explain how you found your answer.

   **c.** Could the quadrilateral have two sides of length 6, one side of length 13.5, and one side of length 1.5? Explain why or why not.

2. Bob has sketched an equilateral triangle. The sum of the lengths of the sides is 12. What is the length of each side of Bob's triangle? Explain your reasoning.

# Additional Practice (continued)

3. Angela has sketched a rectangle. She says that the lengths of the sides of the rectangle add to 26, and the length of one side is 7. What are the length and width of Angela's rectangle? Explain how you found your answer.

4. Use the triangle to answer the following questions.

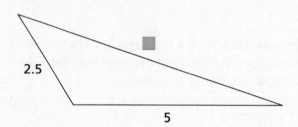

a. Alex estimates that the unknown side length is about 4.5. How do you think Alex's estimate compares with the actual length? Explain your reasoning.

b. Jennifer estimates that the unknown side length is about 8. How do you think Jennifer's estimate compares with the actual length? Explain.

c. Use what you have learned about making triangles with polystrips to estimate the length of the unknown side. Explain why you think your estimate is close to the actual length.

# Additional Practice *(continued)*

**5.** The figure below is made up of squares and triangles. Use the design below and what you know about angle relationships to answer the following questions.

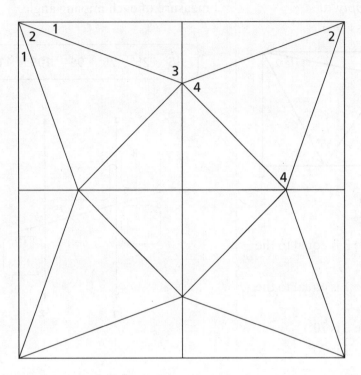

**a.** If the measure of angle 1 is 25°, what is the measure of angle 2? Explain your reasoning.

**b.** If the measure of angle 1 is 25°, what is the measure of angle 3? Explain your reasoning.

**c.** If the measure of angle 1 is 25°, what is the measure of angle 4? Explain your reasoning.

# Additional Practice: Digital Assessments

**6.** In the figure below, two congruent triangles are embedded in squares. Which statements are true? *Select all that apply.*

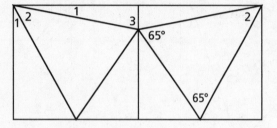

☐ Angle 2 measures 65°.

☐ Angle 1 measures 65°.

☐ The measure of angle 3 is equal to the measure of angle 2.

☐ The measure of angle 1 is equal to the measure of angle 2.

☐ The measure of angle 3 is 70°.

☐ The measure of angle 1 is 70°.

**7.** Two parallel lines are cut by a transversal. Use the values in the bank to label the measure of each missing angle.

15°   25°   75°   95°   105°   110°

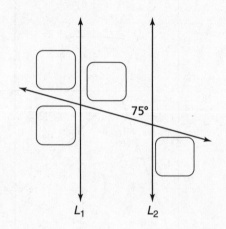

**8.** Write the letter of each shape in the appropriate category. Shapes may belong to more than one category.

A          B          C          D          E          F

| Rotational Symmetry |
| --- |
| |

| Reflectional Symmetry |
| --- |
| |

Tell whether each figure has reflectional symmetry. If it does, draw the line(s) of symmetry. If not, write *none*.

1.
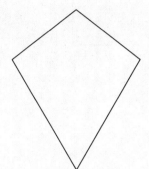

2.

3.
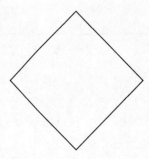

4.
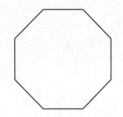

5.
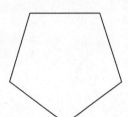

6.

Is there a line of symmetry for each word? If so, draw it.

7. **BOX**

8. **TOOT**

9. **CHICO**

10. **MOM**

Name _____ Date _____ Class _____

# Skill: Rotational Symmetry

Tell whether each figure has rotational symmetry. If it does, tell how many times the figure fits onto itself in one full turn. If not, write *no*.

1.
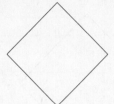

2.
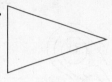

3.

4.

5.

6.
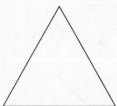

7.
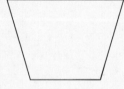

8.

9.

# Skill: Angles and Parallel Lines

**In each diagram below, lines $L_1$ and $L_2$ are parallel lines cut by a transversal. Find the measure of each numbered angle.**

1.
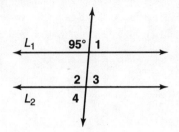

2.
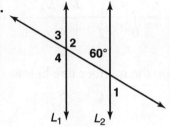

3.
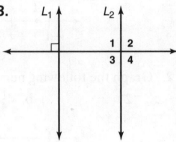

4. Use the figure below. Is line $L_1$ parallel to line $L_2$? Explain how you could use an angle ruler to support your conjecture.

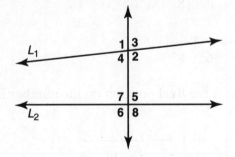

# Additional Practice

1. Estimate the numbers represented by points *A–E*.

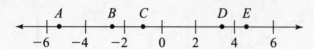

2. Graph the following numbers on the number line below.

   **a.** $^-2$        **b.** $4\frac{1}{4}$        **c.** $^-5.5$        **d.** $\frac{27}{2}$

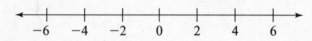

3. Graph each statement on a number line.

   **a.** *x* is greater than $^-2$.        **b.** *x* is less than or equal to 0.

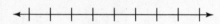 

   **c.** $x > 2$        **d.** $^-6 < x \le 3$

 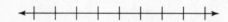

4. Write an inequality for each set of numbers on the number line.

   **a.**
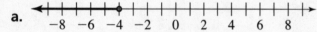

   **b.**
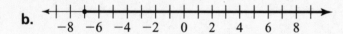

   **c.**
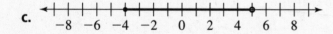

5. For each of the following steps, what is the final position on the number line?

   **a.** Start at $^-6$. Add 7.

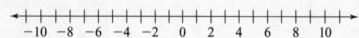

   **b.** Start at 3. Add $^-4$.

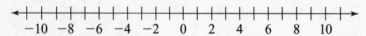

   **c.** Start at 6. Subtract 7.

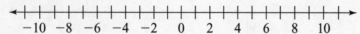

   **d.** Start at $^-4$. Subtract 2.

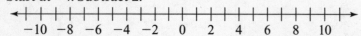

24

# Additional Practice: Digital Assessments

**31.** Which inequality represents the set of numbers represented by this number line?

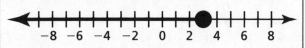

○ $x \leq -3$

○ $x < -3$

○ $x > 3$

○ $x \geq 3$

○ $x \geq 3$

○ $x \geq -3$

**32.** In a trivia contest, Taliyah an ered six questions correctly to earn 6 nts. Then she answered two questions i orrectly and lost 2 points. Circle the te s that show the correct steps and fir position on the number line.

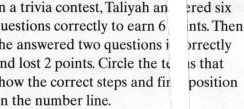

Start at 0. Then $\begin{bmatrix} \text{add} \\ \text{subtract} \\ \text{multiply} \\ \text{divide} \end{bmatrix}$ 6 b oving

6 units $\begin{bmatrix} \text{to the left} \\ \text{to the right} \end{bmatrix}$. Then sub ct 2 by

moving 2 units to the left. The al

position is $\begin{bmatrix} 0 \\ -6 \\ 2 \\ 4 \end{bmatrix}$.

**33.** Shade the circles that show the locations of −6 and its opposite on the number li

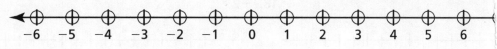

**34.** Order the numbers on the tiles from least to greatest.

| 2 | −1.5 | 3 | −5 | $3\frac{1}{2}$ | $-1\frac{1}{4}$ | 0 |

☐ , ☐ , ☐ , ☐ , ☐ , ☐ , ☐

# Skill: Integers

**Name the integer represented by each point on the number line.**

**1.** A **2.** B **3.** C **4.** D **5.** E **6.** F

**Insert <, >, or = to make a true sentence.**

**7.** $-8$ ☐ $8$     **8.** $4$ ☐ $-4$     **9.** $-8$ ☐ $0$

**10.** $-6$ ☐ $-2$     **11.** $-1$ ☐ $-3$     **12.** $|-4|$ ☐ $0$

**Graph each integer and its opposite on the number line.**

**13.** $-9$     **14.** $5$

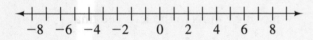 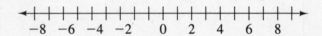

**15.** $6$     **16.** $7$

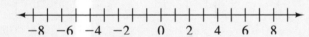

**17.** $8$     **18.** $-2$

 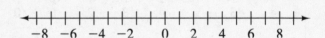

**Order the integers in each set from least to greatest.**

**19.** $0, -5, 5, -15, 15, 25, -25$     **20.** $6, -4, -8, 3, 1, -2, 7$

**21.** $27, -10, -6, -18, 3, 9, -8$     **22.** $-3, -7, 7, 4, -9, -4, -1$

## Skill: Integers (continued)

**Use the information in the graph at the right for Exercises 23–26.**

23. The highest outdoor temperature ever recorded in Nevada, 122°F, was recorded on June 23, 1954. Was it ever that hot in Idaho? Explain.

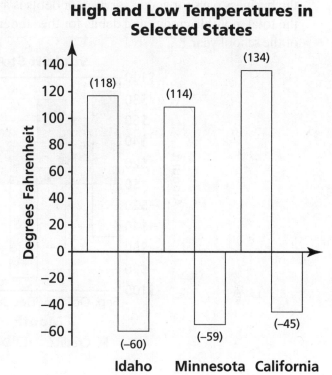

**High and Low Temperatures in Selected States**

24. Which state had a recorded high temperature of 134°F?

25. The lowest temperature ever recorded in Maine, −48°F, was recorded on January 17, 1925. Was it ever that cold in Minnesota? Explain.

26. Which state on the graph had a recorded low temperature of 60°F below zero?

**Write a number sentence to show each result.**

27. The varsity football team gained 7 yards on one play and then lost 4 yards.

28. The airplane descended 140 feet and then rose 112 feet.

29. The squirrel climbed 18 inches up a tree, slipped back 4 inches, and then climbed up 12 inches more.

30. The temperature was 72°F at noon. At midnight a cold front moved in, dropping the temperature 12°F.

# Additional Practice

1. An amount paid to a business for goods or services is a *credit,* and an amount the business pays for goods, services, or debts is a *debit.* The chart below shows the total monthly credits and debits for the student store for the first six months of the school year.

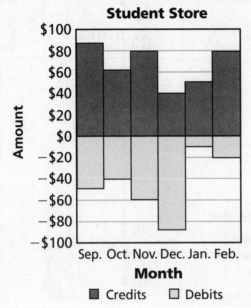

Student Store

Amount / Month

Credits ■   Debits □

**a.** What is the total of the credits for September through February?

**b.** What is the total of the debits for September through February?

**c.** Did the store make or lose money over this time period? Explain your reasoning.

**d.** Adding the credits and debits gives the profit or loss for a given period of time. Tell which months the store showed a loss and which months the store showed a profit. Explain.

**For Exercises 2–4, sketch chips and a chip board. Then, find the difference.**

**2.** $^-8 - 5$          **3.** $3 - 9$          **4.** $^-6 - {^-12}$

# Additional Practice (continued)

**Write both an addition sentence and a subtraction sentence to represent what is shown on the number line.**

**5.**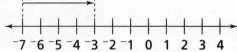

**6.**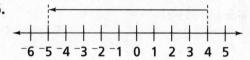

**7.** A chip board has 10 red chips and 10 black chips.

   **a.** What value is represented by this board?

   **b.** If 2 red chips and 2 black chips are removed, what value do the remaining chips represent?

   **c.** If 20 red chips and 20 black chips are added, what value do the chips represent?

**Find the missing value.**

**8.** $\square + 5 = 7$

**9.** $5 + \square = {}^-3$

**10.** $\square + {}^-3 = {}^-9$

**11.** $7 - \square = 3$

**12.** $\square - 10 = {}^-6$

**13.** $7 - \square = 12$

**14.** ${}^-6 - \square = 7$

**15.** ${}^-3.4 - \square = {}^-5.6$

**16.** $\frac{2}{3} - \square = 1$

**17.** $\square - 12 = {}^-5$

**18.** ${}^-4.5 - \frac{9}{2} = \square$

**19.** $3\frac{2}{5} + \square = \frac{2}{5}$

**20.** $\square + 7.6 = 3\frac{3}{5}$

**21.** $\square - {}^-7.8 = 0$

**22.** $\square + \frac{-93}{10} = 10$

## Additional Practice (continued)

**23.** Decide whether the statement is always true, sometimes true, or always false. Explain your reasoning.

   **a.** If a positive integer is subtracted from a negative integer, the difference is a negative integer.

   **b.** If a positive integer is subtracted from a positive integer, the difference is a positive integer.

**24.** Write a complete fact family for each of the following:

   **a.** $^-5 + {}^+2 = {}^-3$               **b.** $^-4 + {}^-6 = {}^-10$

   **c.** $^+0.7 + {}^+0.3 = {}^+1.0$          **d.** $^-3.1 + {}^-1.1 = {}^-4.4$

**25.** Chris said that the fact family for $^-2 + {}^+7 = {}^+5$ should have facts:

$$^-2 + {}^+7 = {}^+5 \qquad\qquad\qquad {}^+5 = {}^-2 + {}^+7$$
$$^+5 - {}^-2 = {}^+7 \qquad\text{and}\qquad {}^+7 = {}^+5 - {}^-2$$
$$^+5 - {}^+7 = {}^-2 \qquad\qquad\qquad {}^-2 = {}^+5 - {}^+7$$

Do you agree? Explain.

# Skill: Subtracting Integers

**Find each difference.**

**1.** $9 - 26$

**2.** ___ 5

**3.** $21 - (-7)$

**4.** $27 - (-16)$

**5.** $-16 - (-43)$

**6.** $47 - 19$

**7.** $-156 - 98$

**8.** $-192 - 47$

**9.** $0 - (-51)$

**10.** $-63 - 89$

**11.** $-12 - (-21)$

**12.** $92 - (\quad)$

**13.** $72 - 15$

**14.** $-86 - (-19)$

**15.** $17 - (-46)$

**16.** $-78 - (-53)$

**17.** $-19 - (-12)$

**18.** $-16 - (-21)$

**19.** $27 - 19$

**20.** $-14 - 27$

# Skill: Adding and Subtracting Rational Numbers Investigation 2

**Accentuate the Negative**

**Find each sum or difference as a mixed number or fraction in simplest form.**

**1.** $\frac{3}{4} + \frac{7}{8}$

**2.** $-1\frac{1}{6} + 2\frac{2}{3}$

**3.** $4\frac{1}{2} - 7\frac{7}{8}$

**4.** $-3\frac{5}{6} - \left(-4\frac{1}{12}\right)$

**5.** $\frac{5}{18} + \frac{7}{12}$

**6.** $-4\frac{7}{20} + 3\frac{9}{10}$

**7.** $5\frac{8}{21} - \left(-3\frac{1}{7}\right)$

**8.** $1\frac{19}{24} + 2\frac{23}{20}$

**9.** $3\frac{16}{25} - 4\frac{7}{20}$

**Write each answer as a fraction or mixed number in simplest form.**

**10.** $14.6 + \left(-3\frac{1}{5}\right)$

**11.** $-7\frac{3}{4} - 4.125$

**12.** $5.75 + \left(-2\frac{1}{8}\right)$

# Additional Practice

**Find the missing value.**

**1.** $\square \times 8 = 56$

**2.** $12 \times \square = {}^-36$

**3.** $\square \times {}^-10 = 90$

**4.** $7 \times \square = {}^-147$

**5.** $\square \div 18 = {}^-54$

**6.** $64 \div \square = 8$

**7.** ${}^-192 \div \square = 16$

**8.** ${}^-99.99 \div \square = {}^-3.03$

**9.** $\frac{2}{3} \times \square = \frac{10}{24}$

**10.** $\square \times 13 = {}^-169$

**11.** ${}^-234 \div 12.5 = \square$

**12.** $3\frac{1}{5} \div \square = {}^-8$

**13.** $\square \times {}^-7.6 = 67.64$

**14.** $\square \div {}^-77.8 = 1$

**15.** $\square \div \frac{{}^-93}{10} = 10$

## Additional Practice *(continued)*

**16.** Write a complete fact family for each of the following:

    **a.** $^-5 \times {}^+2 = {}^-10$

    **b.** $^-4 \times {}^-6 = {}^+24$

    **c.** $^+0.6 \div {}^-0.3 = {}^-2$

    **d.** $^-32 \div {}^-8 = {}^+4$

**17.** For the *Number Line Game* there are three number cubes. Each cube has six sides marked as shown:

    blue number cube: +, +, +, −, −, −

    red number cube: $^-1, {}^-2, {}^-3, {}^-4, {}^-5, {}^-6$

    green number cube: $^+1, {}^+2, {}^+3, {}^+4, {}^+5, {}^+6$

| Juan | Shandra | Kasper |
|---|---|---|
| +, $^-2$, $^+3$ | +, $^-1$, $^+2$ | −, $^-6$, $^+1$ |
| +, $^-4$, $^+1$ | −, $^-5$, $^+2$ | −, $^-1$, $^+4$ |
| −, $^-2$, $^+2$ | −, $^-3$, $^+4$ | +, $^-1$, $^+4$ |
| +, $^-3$, $^+6$ | −, $^-3$, $^+5$ | +, $^-1$, $^+5$ |
| −, $^-2$, $^+6$ | +, $^-6$, $^+6$ | +, $^-4$, $^+4$ |

You start with 0 points. On each turn, you roll the three cubes, multiply the numbers shown on the red and green cubes, and add or subtract the product according to the sign shown on the blue number cube. The winner is the person whose score is closest to 0 after 5 turns.

The table above shows the results for Juan, Shandra, and Kasper. Record the results of each turn for each player in the table below. What is each player's final score? Who won the game?

| | Juan | | Shandra | | Kasper | |
|---|---|---|---|---|---|---|
| | Roll | Score | Roll | Score | Roll | Score |
| Turn 1 | Add −6 | | | | | |
| Turn 2 | | | | | | |
| Turn 3 | | | | | | |
| Turn 4 | | | | | | |
| Turn 5 | | | | | | |

# Additional Practice: Digital Assessments

**18.** A submarine starts at the surface of the Atlantic ocean. It descends 20 feet every minute. Which equation models the submarine's position after an hour?

○ $20 \times 60 = 1{,}200$

○ $20 \times (-60) = -1{,}200$

○ $(-20) \times (-60) = 1{,}200$

○ $(-20) \times (-60) = -1{,}200$

○ $(-20) \times 60 = -1{,}200$

**19.** Write each expression in the appropriate box.

| $6 \div 5$ | $-6 \div 5$ | $6 \div -5$ | $-6 \div -5$ |
| $6 \times 5$ | $-6 \times 5$ | $6 \times -5$ | $-6 \times -5$ |

| **Greater than 1** | **Less than 1** |
| --- | --- |
|  |  |

**20.** Use the tiles provided to find the missing values in each number sentence.

| $-3.3$ | $3.3$ | $6\frac{1}{2}$ | $-\frac{13}{2}$ | $\frac{33}{10}$ | $-12$ | $12$ |

$$\boxed{\phantom{xx}} \times 2 = -13$$

$$\boxed{\phantom{xx}} \div (-1.1) = 3$$

$$\boxed{\phantom{xx}} \div \frac{12}{5} = 5$$

# Skill: Multiplying Integers

**Accentuate the Negative**

**Multiply.**

**1.** $7 \times 8$

**2.** $-5 \times 7$

**3.** $4 \times (-8)$

**4.** $-8 \times (-2)$

**5.** $11 \times (-6)$

**6.** $-7 \times 6$

**7.** $-8 \times (-8)$

**8.** $10 \times 4$

**9.** $21 \times 13$

**10.** $-15 \times 12$

**11.** $-25 \times (-14)$

**12.** $10 \times (-25)$

**For Exercises 13–18, find the missing number.**

**13.** $3 \times \square = -6$

**14.** $4 \times \square = -4$

**15.** $\square \times (-4) = -8$

**16.** $-3 \times \square = 9$

**17.** $-9 \times (-2) = \square$

**18.** $\square \times (-2) = -18$

**19.** Your teacher purchases 24 pastries for a class celebration, at $2 each. What integer expresses the amount he paid?

**20.** Temperatures have been falling steadily at 5°F each day. What integer expresses the change in temperature in degrees 7 days from today?

**21.** A submarine starts at the surface of the Pacific Ocean and descends 60 feet every hour. What integer expresses the submarine's position in feet relative to the surface after 6 hours?

**22.** A skydiver falls at approximately 10 meters per second. Write a number sentence to express how many meters he will fall in 40 seconds.

# Skill: Dividing Integers

**Divide.**

**1.** $14 \div 7$      **2.** $21 \div (-3)$      **3.** $-15 \div 5$

**4.** $-27 \div (-9)$      **5.** $45 \div (-9)$      **6.** $-42 \div 6$

**7.** $-105 \div (-15)$      **8.** $63 \div (-9)$      **9.** $108 \div 6$

**10.** $-204 \div 17$      **11.** $240 \div (-15)$      **12.** $-252 \div (-12)$

**Find each product or quotient.**

**13.** $\dfrac{-36}{9}$      **14.** $\dfrac{-52}{-4}$      **15.** $(-5) \cdot (-20)$

**16.** $\dfrac{-63}{-9}$      **17.** $(-15) \cdot (2)$      **18.** $\dfrac{22}{-2}$

**19.** $(13) \cdot (-6)$      **20.** $\dfrac{-100}{-5}$      **21.** $(-60) \cdot (-3)$

# Skill: Dividing Integers (continued)

**For Exercises 22 and 23, represent each pattern of change with an integer.**

**22.** spends $300 in 5 days

**23.** runs 800 feet in 4 minutes

**24.** Juan's baseball card collection was worth $800. Over the last 5 years, the collection decreased $300 in value. What integer represents the average change in value each year?

**25.** Florence purchased stock for $20 per share. After 6 days, the stock is worth $32 per share. What integer represents the average increase in stock value each day?

# Skill: Multiplying and Dividing Rational Numbers

Accentuate the Negative

**Use the algorithms you developed to find each value.**

**1.** $-\frac{1}{6} \cdot 2\frac{3}{4}$

**2.** $\frac{3}{16} \div \left(-\frac{1}{8}\right)$

**3.** $-\frac{31}{56} \cdot (-8)$

**4.** $-5\frac{7}{12} \div 12$

**5.** $-8 \div \frac{1}{4}$

**6.** $-3\frac{1}{6} \div \left(-2\frac{1}{12}\right)$

**7.** $8\frac{3}{4} \cdot 3\frac{7}{8}$

**8.** $-\frac{11}{12} \div \frac{5}{6}$

**9.** $4\frac{9}{28} \cdot (-7)$

**10.** $-1\frac{1}{15} \div 15$

**11.** $-3 \div \frac{3}{4}$

**12.** $-2\frac{7}{8} \div 3\frac{3}{4}$

**13.** $-\frac{23}{24} \cdot (-8)$

**14.** $\frac{7}{8} \cdot \left(-\frac{2}{7}\right)$

**15.** $-7 \div \frac{1}{9}$

# Additional Practice

1. Find each missing value.

a. $13 - (8 - 2) = 13 - 8 - \square$    b. $-6 - (5 - 3) = -6 - 5 - \square$

c. $12 - (6 - (-1)) = 12 - 6 - \square$    d. $-22 - (-11 - (-4)) = -22 - (-11) - \square$

e. What pattern do you see?

2. Find the correct result for each of the following.

a. $-5 \times 7 + 10 \div 2$    b. $(2 + 4)^2 \times 5 - 2$

c. $3\frac{2}{5} \times 2\frac{1}{2} - 5^3 + 10$    d. $6 \times (3 - 5)^2 + 8$

e. $-6 \times (7 - (-4 + 2))$    f. $-9 \times 8 \div 2^3 + (-5)$

# Additional Practice (continued)

**3.** Find the answers to the following expressions.

**a.** $5 \times 8 \div 2 \div 2$

**b.** $3 + (-5) \times 4 - 2$

**c.** $5 \times 2 \times (-3) + (-12) \div 6$

**d.** $-4 \times (3 + (-10)) - 3^2$

**e.** $(8 - 20) \div 2^2 - 5 \times (-3)$

**f.** $20 - (60 \div (-2 \times 30) - 8) \times 2^2$

**g.** $12 - 8 + 4 - 3$

**h.** $4^2 + \frac{-10}{2} + 13$

**4.** Find each missing value.

**a.** $4 \times 8 + 4 \times 22 = 4 \times \square$

**b.** $-12 \times 43 + (-12) \times (-3) = -12 \times \square$

**c.** $-6 \times \square = (-6) \times 15 + (-6) \times (-5)$

**d.** $-0.4 \times \square = -0.4 \times (-0.7) + (-0.4) \times (-0.3)$

# **Additional Practice** (continued)

**5.** Find each missing value.

  **a.** $2 \times (-7 + 4) = 2 \times (-7) + 2 \times 4 =$ ___ $+$ ___ $=$ ___

  **b.** $1 \times (-7 + 4) =$ ___ $\times (-7) +$ ___ $\times 4 =$ ___ $+$ ___ $=$ ___

  **c.** $0 \times (-7 + 4) =$ ___ $\times (-7) +$ ___ $\times 4 =$ ___ $+$ ___ $=$ ___

  **d.** $-1 \times (-7 + 4) =$ ___ $\times (-7) +$ ___ $\times 4 =$ ___ $+$ ___ $=$ ___

  **e.** $-2 \times (-7 + 4) =$ ___ $\times (-7) +$ ___ $\times 4 =$ ___ $+$ ___ $=$ ___

  **f.** What patterns do you see? Explain your thinking.

**6.** Fill in the missing parts to make the sentences true.

  **a.** $8 \times (6 + 4) = (8 \times$ ___ $) + (8 \times 4)$

  **b.** $7 \times (x + 3) = (7 \times$ ___ $) + ($ ___ $\times 3)$

  **c.** $(-9 \times 5) + ($ ___ $\times 7) = -9 \times ($ ___ $+ 7)$

  **d.** $(x \times 4) + (x \times 5) =$ ___ $\times (4 + 5)$

  **e.** $8x + 12x = x \times ($ ___ $+$ ___ $)$

# Additional Practice

**1.** Refer to the rectangle at the right for the exercises below.

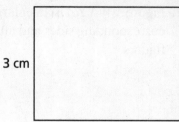

3 cm

4 cm

    **a.** Give the length and width of a larger similar rectangle.
    Explain your reasoning.

    **b.** Give the length and width of a smaller similar rectangle. Explain your
    reasoning.

    **c.** Give the length and width of a rectangle that is *not* similar to this one.
    Explain your reasoning.

# Additional Practice *(continued)*

2. Figure *VWXYZ* is an enlargement of figure *ABCDE*. Name all the pairs of corresponding sides and all the pairs of corresponding angles of the two figures.

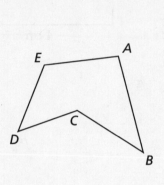 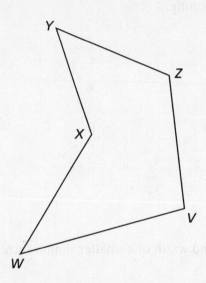

3. **a.** Draw a square. Then draw a square with a side length that is twice the side length of the original square. How many copies of the smaller square will fit inside the larger square?

   **b.** Will you get the same answer for part (a) no matter what side length you choose for the original square? Explain your reasoning.

Name _____ Date _____ Class _____

## Additional Practice (continued)

**4. a.** Carl made shape B by making a photocopy of shape A. What percent did he enter in the copier?

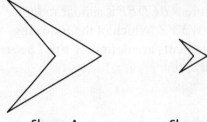

Shape A          Shape B

**b.** Amy made a photocopy of shape A by entering 250% into the photocopier. Sketch the copy she got.

# Additional Practice: Digital Assessments

**5.** Figure *ABCDEF* is similar to figure *UVWXYZ*. Which of the following statements are definitely true? *Select all that apply.*

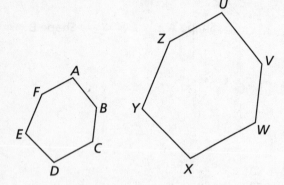

☐ Angle *A* corresponds to angle *U*.
☐ Angle *C* is congruent to angle *W*.
☐ Angle *B* corresponds to angle *Y*.
☐ Side *DE* corresponds to side *XY*.
☐ Side *FE* is the same length as side *WX*.

**6.** Which of the following are equivalent to $\frac{5}{8}$? *Select all that apply.*

☐ $\frac{10}{16}$

☐ $\frac{7}{10}$

☐ $\frac{15}{24}$

☐ 0.625

☐ 0.0625

**7.** Use the tiles to show one way to find 30% of 92.

| 92 | 0.30 | 27.6 | 276 |

| 30 | 0.92 | × | ÷ |

☐ ☐ ☐ = ☐

# Skill: Using Percent

**Find the given percent of each number. Show your work.**

**1.** 20% of 560

**2.** 42% of 200

**3.** 9% of 50

**4.** 40% of 70

**5.** 25% of 80

**6.** 50% of 80

**7.** 40% of 200

**8.** 5% of 80

**9.** 75% of 200

# Additional Practice

1. Draw any rectangle that is not a square. Draw a similar rectangle by applying a scale factor of 3 to the original rectangle.

   a. How many copies of the original rectangle will fit inside the new rectangle?

   b. Will you get the same answer for part (a) no matter what rectangle you use as the original rectangle?

# Additional Practice *(continued)*

2. Make a figure by connecting the following sets of points on the coordinate grid:

   Set 1: $(8, 5), (8, 8), (0, 8), (0, 5), (8, 5)$     Set 2: $(4, 6), (8, 2), (0, 2), (4, 6)$

   Set 3: $(2, 6), (1, 6), (1, 7), (2, 7), (2, 6)$     Set 4: $(6, 6), (7, 6), (7, 7), (6, 7), (6, 6)$

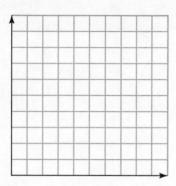

   **a.** Suppose you used the rule $(6x, 6y)$ to transform this figure into a new figure. How would the angles of the new figure compare with the angles of the original? How would the side lengths compare? Would the new figure be similar to the original? Explain.

   **b.** Suppose you used the rule $(3x+1, 3y-4)$ to transform the original figure into a new figure. Would the new figure be similar to the original? Explain.

**Additional Practice** (continued)

3. Recall that Zug Wump was made from Mug Wump using a scale factor of 2. What is the scale factor from Zug to Mug? Explain.

4. a. Wendy drew a very large Wump using the rule $(8x, 8y)$. She said that the scale factor from Mug to her Wump was 8 and that the scale factor from Zug to her Wump was 4. Do you agree with Wendy? Explain.

   b. Wendy could not figure out the scale factor from Bug Wump to her new large Wump. What is this scale factor? (Hint: Applying the rule $(3x, 3y)$ to Mug creates Bug.)

# Additional Practice: Digital Assessments

**5.** The original figure below is transformed using the rule $(x - 1, 2y)$.

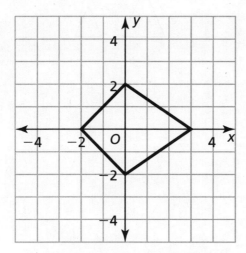

Which of these points are vertices of the new transformed figure? *Select all that apply.*

☐ $(2, 0)$

☐ $(2, -1)$

☐ $(-1, -4)$

☐ $(-3, 0)$

☐ $(-3, -1)$

☐ $(1, 0)$

☐ $(-1, 4)$

**6.** Write the letter for each pair of figures in the correct box.

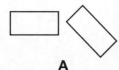

**A**

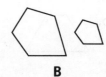

**B**

**C**

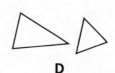

**D**

| Similar Figures |
| --- |
|  |

| Not Similar Figures |
| --- |
|  |

# Skill: Similar Figures

**Tell whether the triangles are *similar*.**

1.

2.

3.

4. List the pairs of figures that appear to be similar.

a.

b.

c.

d.

e.

f. ▫

g. ▽

h.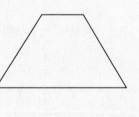

# Skill: Similar Figures (continued)

**For Exercises 5 and 6, graph quadrilateral *ABCD*. Then graph its image *A′B′C′D′* with the given scale factor.**

**5.** $A(2, -2), B(3, 2), C(-3, 2), D(-2, -2)$; scale factor 2

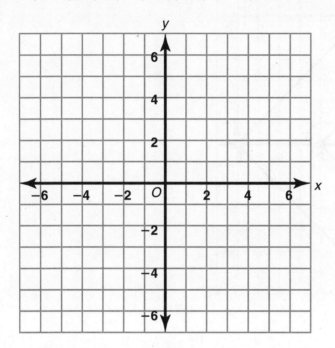

**6.** $A(6, 3), B(0, 6), C(-6, 2), D(-6, -5)$; scale factor $\frac{1}{2}$

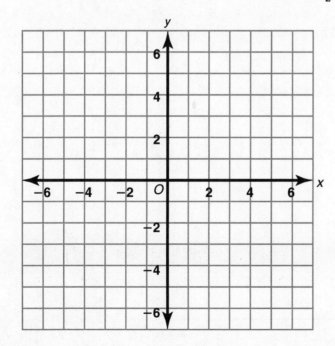

## Skill: Similar Figures (continued)

**7.** Quadrilateral $A'B'C'D'$ is similar to quadrilateral $ABCD$. Find the scale factor from $ABCD$ to $A'B'C'D'$.

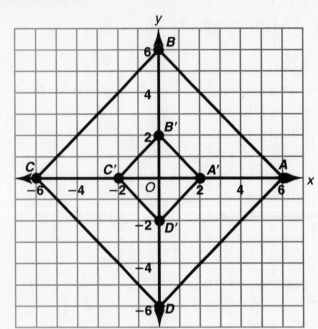

# Additional Practice

**1.** On the grid below, make a right triangle with legs of length 8 and 12.

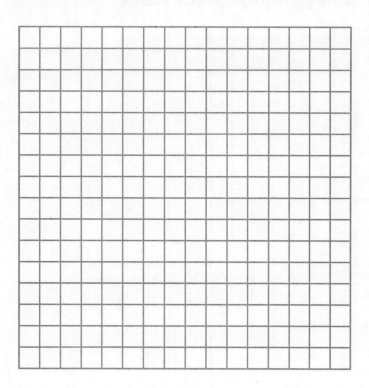

**a.** Give the leg lengths of two smaller right triangles that are similar to the one you drew and that have whole-number side lengths.

**b.** Copies of each smaller triangle can be put together to exactly match the original triangle. How many of each smaller triangle does it take to match the original?

# Additional Practice (continued)

**2.** In the grid below, each unit represents 1 centimeter. On the grid, make an isosceles triangle with base and height both equal to 6 centimeters.

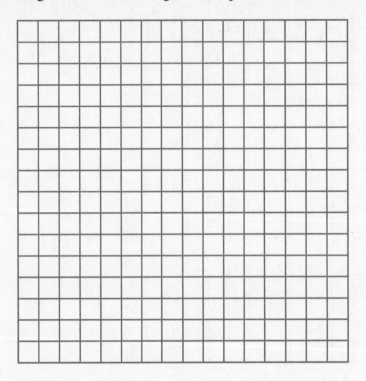

**a.** Can isosceles triangles with base and height equal to 2 centimeters be put together to exactly match the shape of the original triangle? Is each smaller triangle similar to the original?

**b.** Can isosceles triangles with base and height equal to 4 centimeters be put together to exactly match the shape of the original triangle? Is each smaller triangle similar to the original?

# Additional Practice (continued)

**3.** Find the missing side lengths in each pair of similar figures below.

**a.**

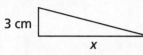

**b.**

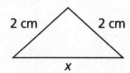

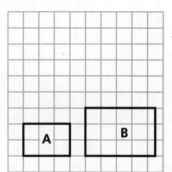

**4.** For each pair of similar figures below, give the scale factor from figure A to figure B.

**a.**

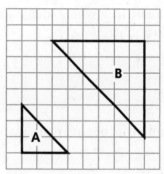

**b.**

**c.**

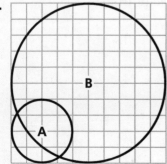

## Additional Practice (continued)

**5. a.** The drawing below shows how a square foot and a square yard compare. How many square feet are in a square yard? Explain your reasoning.

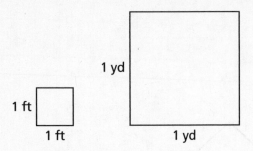

**b.** Are a square foot and a square yard similar? If so, what is the scale factor from a square foot to a square yard? What is the scale factor from a square yard to a square foot?

**c.** Compare a square inch with a square foot. What is the scale factor from a square inch to a square foot?

**d.** How many square inches are in a square foot? Explain.

**e.** Compare a square inch with a square yard. What is the scale factor from a square inch to a square yard?

**f.** How many square inches are in a square yard?

# Additional Practice: Digital Assessments

**6.** The figures below are similar. Use the values in the bank to label the missing side lengths.

> 12   15   16.5   18   32.5   36

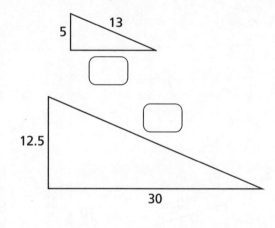

**7.** The two pentagons below are similar. Complete the missing side lengths using the values in the bank.

> $\frac{1}{3}$ in.  $\frac{2}{3}$ in.  $\frac{4}{3}$ in.  1 in.  2 in.  3 in.  4 in.

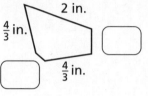

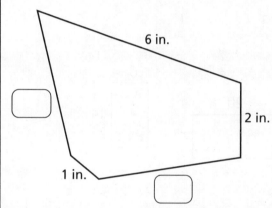

**8.** Triangle $ABC$ is similar to triangle $A'B'C'$. Circle the numbers that make the statements true.

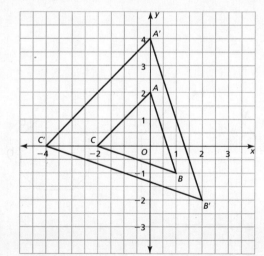

The scale factor from triangle $ABC$ to triangle $A'B'C'$ is $\begin{bmatrix} 2 \\ 4 \\ \frac{1}{2} \\ \frac{1}{4} \end{bmatrix}$ because the coordinates of each vertex are multiplied by $\begin{bmatrix} 2 \\ 4 \\ \frac{1}{2} \\ \frac{1}{4} \end{bmatrix}$.

**9.** Rectangle $A$ is a transformation of rectangle $B$, scaled by a factor of 4. How many copies of rectangle $B$ can fit inside rectangle $A$?

    ○ 2      ○ 4      ○ 8      ○ 16

# Skill: Similar Polygons

**The pairs of figures below are similar. Find the value of each variable.**

**1.**

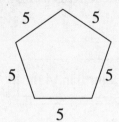

**2.**

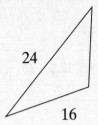

**3.**

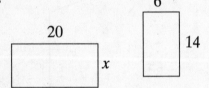

**4.**

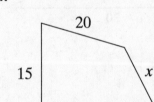

**5.**

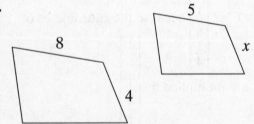

**6.**

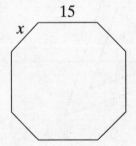

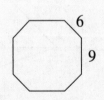

# Skill: Fractions, Decimals, and Percents

**Write three equivalent fractions for each fraction.**

**1.** $\frac{3}{10}$

**2.** $\frac{7}{8}$

**3.** $\frac{5}{6}$

**4.** $\frac{3}{4}$

**5.** $\frac{15}{20}$

**6.** $\frac{8}{12}$

**7.** $\frac{15}{45}$

**8.** $\frac{8}{32}$

**Write each fraction as a decimal and as a percent.**

**9.** $\frac{3}{5}$

**10.** $\frac{7}{10}$

**11.** $\frac{13}{25}$

**12.** $\frac{17}{20}$

# Additional Practice

**1. a.** Rachel was working with the triangles below:

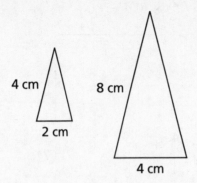

She wrote the fraction $\frac{1}{2}$. What was she thinking about?

**b.** Next, she wrote the fraction $\frac{1}{3}$ while working with these two triangles:

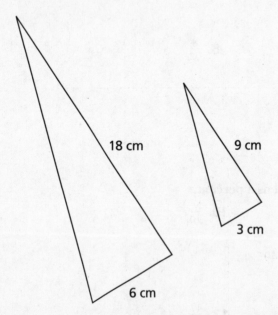

Was she thinking in the same way or differently? Explain.

# Additional Practice (continued)

**2.** Below are several pairs of similar figures. In each, find the missing measurement(s).

**a.**

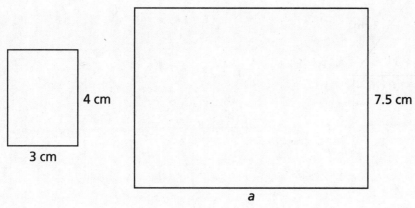

**b.**

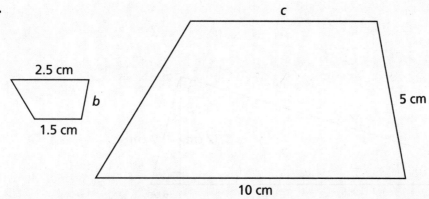

**c.**

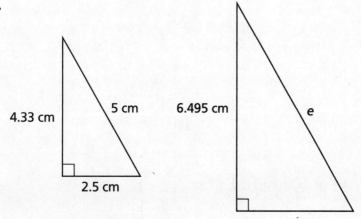

# Additional Practice (continued)

**3.** In each figure below, find the missing measurement.

**a.**

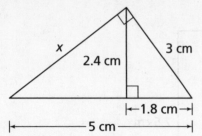

**b.**

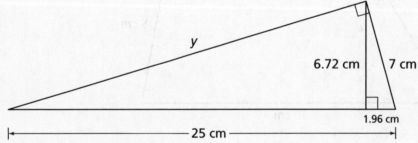

# Additional Practice: Digital Assessments

**4.** Using the values from the bank, find the missing measurement.

> 5 cm   6 cm   10 cm   12 cm   18 cm

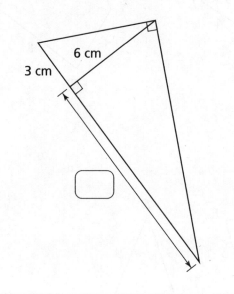

**5.** Which statements about the figures are true? *Select all that apply.*

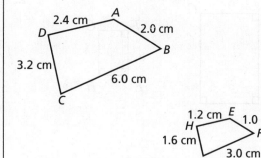

☐ *ABCD* is similar to *EFGH*.

☐ Side *AB* is congruent to side *EF*.

☐ Side *DC* corresponds to side *HG*.

☐ The ratio of side *AB* to side *AD* is the same as the ratio of side *EF* to side *EH*.

☐ The scale factor from *ABCD* to *EFGH* is 2.

**6.** Jaqué wants to calculate the scale factor for the pair of similar figures. Explain how she can determine the scale factor from the figure on the left to the figure on the right.

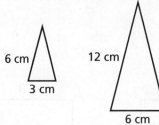

First, she must identify the $\begin{bmatrix} \text{congruent} \\ \text{equivalent} \\ \text{corresponding} \\ \text{identical} \\ \text{matching} \end{bmatrix}$ sides.

Because one side of length 12 cm corresponds

to a side of length $\begin{bmatrix} 12\ \text{cm} \\ 6\ \text{cm} \\ 3\ \text{cm} \end{bmatrix}$, she divides 12 by $\begin{bmatrix} 12 \\ 6 \\ 3 \end{bmatrix}$.

The result shows that the scale factor is $\begin{bmatrix} 4 \\ 3 \\ 2 \\ \frac{1}{2} \end{bmatrix}$.

# Skill: Similarity and Ratios

**Tell whether each pair of polygons is similar. Explain why or why not.**

**1.**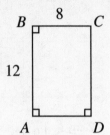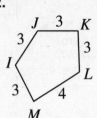

**2.**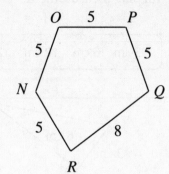

**3.**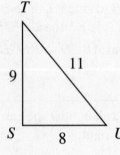

**4.**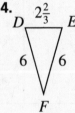

**5.**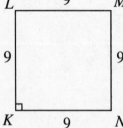

**6.**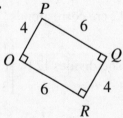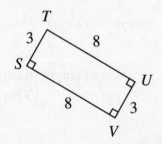

# Skill: Similarity and Ratios (continued)

**Exercise 7–11 show pairs of similar polygons. Find the missing side lengths.**

**7.**

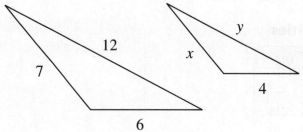

**8.**

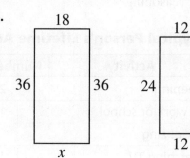

**9.**

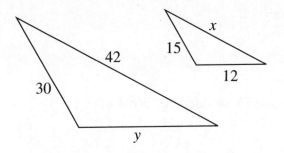

**10.**

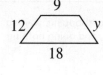

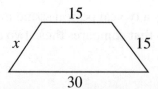

**11.**

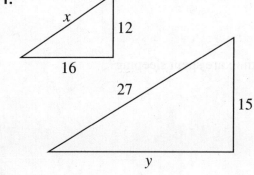

# Additional Practice

1. **a.** According to the table, how long is a typical person's lifetime? Explain your reasoning.

### Typical Person's Lifetime Activities

| Activity | Number of Years |
|---|---|
| Sleeping | 24.5 |
| At work or school | 13.5 |
| Socializing | 4.5 |
| Watching TV | 12 |
| Reading | 3 |
| Eating | 3 |
| Bathing and grooming | 1.75 |
| Talking on the telephone | 1 |
| Miscellaneous activities* | 9.5 |

\* Such as housekeeping, shopping, waiting in lines, walking, driving, entertainment, and doing nothing

**b.** Does a typical person spend more years watching TV or sleeping? Write a ratio that compares these two amounts.

**c.** The number of years spent doing miscellaneous activities is about how many times the number of years spent socializing?

**d.** What percent of the total number of years in a lifetime are spent sleeping? What percent are spent at work or school?

**e.** About what fraction of a lifetime is spent watching TV and talking on the phone? What fraction is spent in miscellaneous activities?

## Additional Practice (continued)

**2. a.** This table shows the typical weight of various parts of the body for an adult weighing 152 pounds. Estimate the percent of the total body weight for each part. Explain your reasoning.

| Body Part | Weight (lb) |
|---|---|
| Head | 10.5 |
| Neck and Trunk | 70.0 |
| Arms | 16.5 |
| Hands | 2.5 |
| Legs | 47.5 |
| Feet | 5.0 |

**b.** Make a circle graph that shows the percent of the total body weight for each body part.

**c.** The neck, trunk, and legs account for what total percent of the body weight?

# Additional Practice (continued)

**3. a.** Of the 756 students in Chad's middle school, 44% participate in sports, 29% play in the band, and 37% take the bus to school. How many students in Chad's middle school play in the band? Explain your reasoning.

**b.** How many students in Chad's middle school take the bus to school?

**c.** If you add up the percents of students who play sports, play in the band, and take the bus to school, you get 110%. Explain why the percents do not add to 100%.

**4. a.** Of the students in Ms. Yadav's fourth-period math class, 16 are wearing athletic shoes, 10 are wearing boots, and 4 are wearing other kinds of shoes. What fraction of Ms. Yadav's students are wearing boots? Explain.

**b.** Suppose 1,006 students attend the middle school where Ms. Yadav teaches. Use your answer from part (a) to estimate the number of students who are wearing boots. Explain.

## Additional Practice (continued)

**5. a.** Use the table below. About what fraction of the total number of endangered species are found only in foreign countries?

**Numbers of Endangered Species**

|  | United States Only | United States and Foreign | Foreign Only |
|---|---|---|---|
| **Animals** | 262 | 51 | 493 |
| **Plants** | 378 | 10 | 1 |
| **Total** | 640 | 61 | 494 |

**b.** How many times more endangered plant species are there in the United States than in foreign countries? Explain your reasoning.

**c.** About what percent of the total number of endangered animals lives only in the United States?

**d.** What is the ratio of Endangered Plants to Endangered Animals in the United States only? In foreign countries only?

**e.** What is the difference between the number of endangered animals in the United States and foreign countries and the number of endangered plants in the United States and foreign countries?

# Additional Practice: Digital Assessments

**6.** The table shows the number of students who are wearing each color shirt.

| Color of Shirt | Number of Students |
|---|---|
| Blue | 9 |
| Green | 4 |
| Red | 6 |
| White | 4 |
| Yellow | 2 |

Shade the section of the circle graph that represents the portion of students wearing a red shirt.

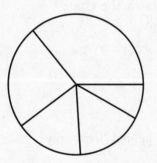

**7.** The table represents the results of a survey that asked the 11th and 12th graders which sport is their favorite. Circle the values that make each statement true.

|  | Soccer | Football | Cross Country |
|---|---|---|---|
| 11th grade | 29 | 25 | 12 |
| 12th grade | 22 | 18 | 24 |

**a.** The total number of students who took

the survey is $\begin{bmatrix} 43 \\ 51 \\ 64 \\ 66 \\ 130 \end{bmatrix}$.

**b.** The ratio of 11th-grade students to 12th-grade students who chose football as

their favorite sport is $\begin{bmatrix} 18 \\ 22 \\ 25 \\ 29 \\ 43 \end{bmatrix}$ to $\begin{bmatrix} 18 \\ 22 \\ 25 \\ 29 \\ 43 \end{bmatrix}$.

**c.** The percentage of cross country fans that are 11th-grade students is about

$\begin{bmatrix} 25\% \\ 33\% \\ 50\% \\ 67\% \\ 75\% \end{bmatrix}$.

**8.** There are 56 students who regularly volunteer at a homeless shelter. Approximately 22% of them are elementary students, 27% of them are middle school students, and 51% are high school students. Approximately how many of the students are middle school students?

○ 12  ○ 27

○ 15  ○ 56

○ 28

# Skill: Writing Ratios

**Write three ratios that each diagram can represent.**

1.

2.

**The table below shows the results of a survey. Write a ratio for each comparison.**

### Which Meal Do You Want for the Party?

| Tacos | Pizza |
|-------|-------|
| ✝✝✝ ‖‖ ✝✝✝ | ✝✝✝ ✝✝✝ ✝✝✝ ╎ |

3. *Tacos* to *Pizza*

4. *Pizza* to *Tacos*

5. *Tacos* to the total

6. *Pizza* to the total

# Skill: Writing Ratios (continued)

The table below shows the results when the seventh-grade classes were asked whether they wanted chicken or pasta served at their awards banquet. Use the table for Exercises 7–8.

**Banquet Preferences**

| Room Number | Chicken | Pasta |
|---|---|---|
| 201 | 10 | 12 |
| 202 | 8 | 17 |
| 203 | 16 | 10 |

7. In Room 201, what is the ratio of students who prefer chicken to students who prefer pasta?

8. Combine the totals for all three rooms. What is the ratio of the number of students who prefer pasta to the number of students who prefer chicken?

9. A bag contains 8 yellow marbles and 6 blue marbles. What number of yellow marbles can you add to the bag so that the ratio of yellow to blue marbles is 2 : 1?

# Skill: Ratios and Fractions

**Write each ratio in simplest form.**

1. $\frac{2}{6}$　　　　　　　　　2. $3:21$

3. 16 to 20　　　　　　　4. $\frac{3}{30}$

5. 12 to 18　　　　　　　6. $81:27$

7. $\frac{6}{28}$　　　　　　　　8. 49 to 14

**Compare each pair of numbers. Use <, >, or =.**

9. $\frac{7}{8}$ ☐ $\frac{3}{30}$　　　　　　10. $\frac{4}{5}$ ☐ $\frac{1}{2}$

11. $\frac{6}{12}$ ☐ $\frac{4}{8}$　　　　　　12. $\frac{7}{15}$ ☐ $\frac{11}{15}$

13. $\frac{4}{5}$ ☐ $\frac{6}{10}$　　　　　　14. $\frac{7}{12}$ ☐ $\frac{2}{3}$

15. $\frac{8}{15}$ ☐ $\frac{1}{2}$　　　　　　16. $\frac{10}{15}$ ☐ $\frac{8}{12}$

17. $\frac{4}{9}$ ☐ $\frac{7}{9}$　　　　　　18. $\frac{2}{5}$ ☐ $\frac{3}{8}$

19. $\frac{1}{2}$ ☐ $\frac{11}{20}$　　　　　20. $\frac{7}{16}$ ☐ $\frac{1}{2}$

# Additional Practice

**1. a.** Bill has a paper route. It takes him 50 minutes to deliver newspapers to his 40 customers. How long will it take Bill to complete his route if he adds 20 more customers in his neighborhood? Explain.

**b.** Only 30 of Bill's 40 customers take the Sunday paper. About how long does it take Bill to deliver his papers on Sundays?

**2.** A micron is a metric unit of length. There are 1 million (1,000,000) microns in 1 meter.

**a.** How many microns equal 1 centimeter? Explain.

**b.** An object has a length of 2,911 microns. What is the length of the object in centimeters?

**c.** An object has a width of 0.000351 meter. What is the width of the object in microns?

**d.** Which metric unit—meters, centimeters, or microns—do you think is best to use to express the length of your pencil? Explain.

## Additional Practice *(continued)*

**3.** Betty and Derek are making punch for a class party. The directions on the liquid punch mix say to use 3 cups of mix for every 7 cups of water. Betty and Derek want to make enough punch so that each of the 25 people at the party can have 2 cups.

  **a.** How many cups of punch mix will Betty and Derek need to use? Explain.

  **b.** Betty and Derek want to put the punch in bowls that hold 20 cups each. How many bowls will they need?

**4.** Use the diagrams below.

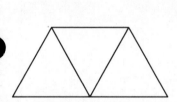 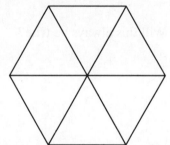 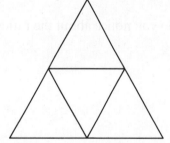

  **a.** What is the ratio of the area of the trapezoid to the area of the hexagon? Explain your reasoning.

  **b.** What is the ratio of the area of the large triangle to the area of the hexagon? Explain.

  **c.** If the area of the hexagon is 24 square units, what is the area of the trapezoid? What is the area of the large triangle? Explain.

# Additional Practice (continued)

**5.** Gabrielle, Hannah, and Gavin decide to share 12 cookies between them, so each of them gets 4. When another friend Blake joins them, they decide to share the 12 cookies, so that each person gets 3.

**a.** Use a ratio to compare numbers of people before and after Blake arrives.

**b.** Use a ratio to compare the number of cookies in each share before and after Blake arrives.

**c.** What do you notice about the ratios? Will this always be true?

**6.** Josh jogs an average of 8 miles per week for three weeks.

**a.** At this rate, how many miles will he jog in 52 weeks?

**b.** How many miles will he need to jog during the fourth week to bring his four-week average to 10 miles per week? Explain your reasoning.

# Additional Practice (continued)

**7.** Tony can type at a constant rate of 55 words per minute.

   **a.** Write an equation for the number of words $W$ Tony can type in $T$ minutes.

   **b.** How many words can Tony type in 20 minutes?

   **c.** If Tony has a half hour to type a 1,600-word essay, will he have time to type the entire essay? Explain your reasoning.

**8.** A veterinarian's clinic has a patient load of 150 cats and dogs. The ratio of cats to dogs is 4 to 8. How many patients are cats and how many are dogs? Explain your reasoning.

**9.** On a map, 1 centimeter = 50 kilometers. What is the actual distance between two towns that are 3.5 centimeters apart on the map? Explain your reasoning.

## Additional Practice (continued)

**10.** Kyle has maintained a consistent batting average of 0.350 on the Metropolis Middle School baseball team during the first half of the season. Assuming his batting average stays the same for the rest of the season, write and solve proportions to answer parts (a)–(d).

   **a.** How many hits should Kyle make in his next 20 times at bat?

   **b.** How many hits should Kyle make in his next 35 times at bat?

   **c.** How many times at bat should it take Kyle to make 10 hits?

   **d.** How many times at bat should it take Kyle to make 18 hits?

## Additional Practice (continued)

11. In a home-run derby contest after the little league baseball session had ended, 4 of Calvin's 12 hits were home runs. Suppose Calvin's success rate stays about the same for his next 100 hits. Write and solve proportions to answer parts (a)–(d).

    **a.** About how many home runs will Calvin make out of his next 48 hits?

    **b.** About how many home runs will Calvin make out of his next 84 hits?

    **c.** About how many hits will it take for Calvin to hit 8 more home runs?

    **d.** About how many hits will it take for him to make 36 more home runs?

# Additional Practice (continued)

**12.** The Elsie Dairy uses a machine that fills 16 cartons of milk each minute.

  **a.** Complete the table below.

| Time (min) | 0 | 1 | 2 | 4 | 10 | 12 | 24 | 60 |
|---|---|---|---|---|---|---|---|---|
| Cartons of Milk | 0 | | | | | | | |

  **b.** Write an equation that expresses the relationship between the number of cartons $C$ and the number of minutes $M$.

  **c.** What is the constant of proportionality in your equation from part (b)?

  **d.** Write two unit rates relating the number of minutes and number of cartons of milk.

## **Additional Practice** *(continued)*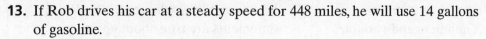

**13.** If Rob drives his car at a steady speed for 448 miles, he will use 14 gallons of gasoline.

   **a.** Make a rate table to show the number of miles he can drive his car for 1, 2, 3, 4, . . , and 10 gallons of gas.

   **b.** Write an equation that expresses the relationship between the number of miles driven, $m$, in terms of the number of gallons of gasoline used, $g$.

   **c.** What is the constant of proportionality in your equation from part (b)?

   **d.** Rob drives his car at the same steady speed and uses 22 gallons of gas. How many miles has he driven?

# Additional Practice: Digital Assessments

**14.** Quinn can read 6 pages in 2 minutes. Circle the correct numbers and variables to create an equation that shows the relationship between the time, $t$, and the number of pages, $P$, if Quinn reads at a constant pace.

$$\begin{bmatrix} P \\ t \end{bmatrix} = \begin{bmatrix} 0 \\ 1 \\ 2 \\ 3 \\ 6 \end{bmatrix} \begin{bmatrix} P \\ t \end{bmatrix}$$

**15.** Jairo bought 5 apples for $3.00. Which statements are true about apple purchases? *Select all that apply.*

☐ 2 apples cost $1.20

☐ 3 apples cost $1.60

☐ 4 apples cost $2.50

☐ 7 apples cost $4.20

☐ 10 apples cost $6.00

**16.** Write each proportion in the box with the solution.

$$\frac{12}{20} = \frac{3}{x} \qquad \frac{6}{12} = \frac{x}{8} \qquad \frac{3}{6} = \frac{2}{x} \qquad \frac{8}{6} = \frac{x}{3} \qquad \frac{x}{15} = \frac{3}{9}$$

| $x = 5$ |
|---|
|  |

| $x = 4$ |
|---|
|  |

**17.** Write each situation in the box with the correct unit rate.

travel 50 miles in 2 hours     travel 120 miles in 6 hours     travel 100 miles in 4 hours

travel 100 miles in 5 hours     travel 180 miles in 9 hours

| 25 Miles per Hour |
|---|
|  |

| 20 Miles per Hour |
|---|
|  |

# Skill: Finding and Using Rates

**Write the unit rate for each situation.**

**1.** travel 250 miles in 5 hours

**2.** earn $75.20 in 8 hours

**3.** read 80 pages in 2 hours

**4.** type 8,580 words in 2 hours 45 minutes

**5.** manufacture 2,488 parts in 8 hours

**6.** 50 copies of a book on 2 shelves

**7.** $30 for 6 books

**8.** 24 points in 3 games

**For exercises 9–10, find each unit price. Then determine the better buy.**

**9.** paper: 100 sheets for $0.99
           500 sheets for $4.29

**10.** peanuts: 1 pound for $1.29
             12 ounces for $0.95

Name _____ Date _____ Class _____

# Skill: Finding and Using Rates (continued)

**For Exercises 11–14, find each unit price. Then determine the better buy.**

**11.** crackers: 15 ounces for $1.79
12 ounces for $1.49

**12.** apples: 3 pounds for $1.89
5 pounds for $2.49

**13.** mechanical pencils: 4 for $1.25
25 for $5.69

**14.** bagels: 4 for $0.89
6 for $1.39

**15. a.** Yolanda and Yoko ran in a 100-yard dash. When Yolanda crossed the finish line in 15 seconds, Yoko was 10 yards behind her. The girls then repeated the race, with Yolanda starting 10 yards behind the starting line. If each girl ran at the same rate as before, who won the race? By how many yards?

**b.** Assume the girls run at the same rate as before. How far behind the starting line should Yolanda be in order for the two to finish in a tie?

# Skill: Finding and Using Rates (continued)

**16.** During the breaststroke competitions of a recent Olympics, Nelson Diebel swam 100 meters in 62 seconds, and Mike Bowerman swam 200 meters in 130 seconds. Who swam at a faster rate?

**17.** During a vacation, the Vasquez family traveled 174 miles in 3 hours on Monday, and 290 miles in 5 hours on Tuesday. Write an equation relating miles $m$ traveled to hours $h$.

# Skill: Solving Proportions

**Solve each proportion for the missing value.**

**1.** $\dfrac{k}{8} = \dfrac{14}{4}$

**2.** $\dfrac{u}{3} = \dfrac{10}{5}$

**3.** $\dfrac{14}{6} = \dfrac{d}{15}$

**4.** $\dfrac{5}{1} = \dfrac{m}{4}$

**5.** $\dfrac{36}{32} = \dfrac{n}{8}$

**6.** $\dfrac{5}{30} = \dfrac{1}{x}$

**7.** $\dfrac{t}{4} = \dfrac{5}{10}$

**8.** $\dfrac{9}{2} = \dfrac{v}{4}$

**9.** $\dfrac{x}{10} = \dfrac{6}{4}$

**10.** $\dfrac{8}{12} = \dfrac{2}{b}$

**11.** $\dfrac{v}{15} = \dfrac{4}{6}$

**12.** $\dfrac{3}{18} = \dfrac{2}{s}$

**Estimate the solution of each proportion.**

**13.** $\dfrac{m}{25} = \dfrac{16}{98}$

**14.** $\dfrac{7}{3} = \dfrac{52}{n}$

**15.** $\dfrac{30}{5.9} = \dfrac{k}{10}$

**16.** $\dfrac{2.8}{j} = \dfrac{1.3}{2.71}$

**17.** $\dfrac{y}{12} = \dfrac{2.89}{4.23}$

**18.** $\dfrac{5}{8} = \dfrac{b}{63}$

# Skill: Solving Proportions (continued)

**19.** A contractor estimates it will cost $2,400 to build a deck to a customer's specifications. How much would it cost to build five more identical decks?

**20.** A recipe requires 3 cups of flour to make 27 dinner rolls. How much flour is needed to make 9 rolls?

**21.** Mandy runs 4 kilometers in 18 minutes. She plans to run in a 15-kilometer race. How long will it take her to complete the race if she runs at the same pace?

**22.** Ken's new car can go 26 miles per gallon of gasoline. The car's gasoline tank holds 14 gallons. How far will he be able to go on a full tank?

**23.** Eleanor can complete two skirts in 15 days. How long will it take her to complete eight skirts?

**24.** Three eggs are required to make two dozen muffins. How many eggs are needed to make 12 dozen muffins?

# Additional Practice

**For Exercises 1–5, find the tax. Round to the nearest cent.**

**1.** a fiction novel for $18.99 at 6% sales tax

**2.** an electronic tablet for $155.49 at 8% sales tax

**3.** a one-night hotel stay for $77.50 at 3% lodging tax

**4.** a pair of shoes for $65.19 at 5% sales tax

**5.** a weekly income of $575 at 14% income tax

**Additional Practice** *(continued)*

6. A soccer team eats lunch at a restaurant on the way to a tournament. The total cost of the food was $85.25 before 6% tax and 18% tip.

   **a.** What was the tax added to the bill?

   **b.** What was the tip left for the servers? The tip is computed on the amount before the tax.

   **c.** What is the ratio of the amount of tip to the amount of the tax? How does this relate to the ratio of their percents?

   **d.** What was the total cost of lunch at the restaurant?

# Additional Practice (continued)

7. Melissa wants to purchase a digital camera. The listed price of the camera is $195.99. The camera is on sale for 10% off and Melissa has a coupon for 5% off. Sales tax is 7%.

   **a.** How much money will the 10% off sale save Melissa?

   **b.** The coupon is applied to the sale price of the camera. How much will Melissa save by using the coupon?

   **c.** Sales tax is applied after all discounts are given. How much will Melissa pay for the camera?

# Additional Practice (continued)

**For Exercises 8–11, use the following information.**

A sporting goods store sells new and used boats. The markup on the boats is 75%.
A salesperson who sells a boat earns a 30% commission on the markup amount.

**8.** Complete the table.

| Buying Price | Markup | Selling Price | Commission | Store Profit |
|---|---|---|---|---|
| $1,000 | | | | |
| $4,000 | | | | |
| $2,500 | | | | |
| $6,400 | | | | |
| | | $8,000 | | |
| | | $10,000 | | |
| | | | $1,000 | |

**9.** Write an equation that shows a salesperson's commission $C$ given the selling price $S$ of a boat.

**10.** Write an equation that shows how the store can determine its profit $P$ based on the cost $B$ in purchasing a boat.

**11.** The store marks down the selling price of a boat 30% for a clearance sale. If the original selling price is $7,500, what commission will the salesperson earn for selling the boat at the clearance price? Write an equation that uses the original selling price $S$ of the boat to determine the commission $C$ earned for the boat sold at clearance.

# Additional Practice (continued)

**For Exercises 12–14, use the following information for converting units of area.**

| | |
|---|---|
| 1 square foot = 144 square inches | 1 board = 12 square inches |
| 1 square yard = 9 square feet | 1 cord = 192 boards |
| 1 acre = 4,840 square yards | 1 rood = 1,210 square yards |
| 1 barony = 4,000 acres | 1 square chain = 484 square yards |

**12. a.** How many boards are in 1 square foot?

   **b.** How many boards are in 1 square yard?

**13. a.** How many square inches are in 1 cord?

   **b.** Which is bigger, a square yard or a cord? By how many more square inches?

**14. a.** How many roods are in 1 acre?

   **b.** How many square chains are in 1 acre?

# Additional Practice (continued)

**For Exercises 15–16, use the following information for converting units of area.**

| | |
|---|---|
| 1 square foot = 144 square inches | 1 board = 12 square inches |
| 1 square yard = 9 square feet | 1 cord = 192 boards |
| 1 acre = 4,840 square yards | 1 rood = 1,210 square yards |
| 1 barony = 4,000 acres | 1 square chain = 484 square yards |

**15. a.** There are 3,097,600 square yards in 1 square mile. Which is bigger, a square mile or a barony? How many square yards is the difference?

   **b.** How many boards are in 1 square yard?

**16.** A landscaping company charges $0.01 per square foot for 3 months of mowing.

   **a.** What is the charge per square yard?

   **b.** What is the charge per acre?

   **c.** What would be the charge to a business with 48.5 acres of land?

# Additional Practice (continued)

**For Exercises 17–19, use the following information.**

**The table shows some recipes for organic plant foods.**

| Green Tea Recipe | Gelatin (for Nitrogen) | Epsom Salt |
|---|---|---|
| 20% Green Tea | 10% Gelatin | 1% Epsom Salt |
| 80% Water | 90% Water | 99% Water |

**17.** Complete the table to show the unit rates for the ingredients in the Green Tea Recipe.

| Cups of Green Tea | | | 1 |
|---|---|---|---|
| Cups of Water | | 1 | |
| Total Cups in Mix | 100 | | |

**18.** Write two equations relating the number of cups of green tea $G$ and the number of cups of water $W$ in the green tea plant food recipe.

**19. a.** Linda calculates that she uses 55 cups of mix to feed all of her plants. How many cups each of green tea and water does she need to make enough mixture?

**b.** Describe two ways to solve part (a).

# Additional Practice (continued)

**For Exercises 20–22, use the following information.**

**The table shows some recipes for organic plant foods.**

| Green Tea Recipe | Gelatin (for Nitrogen) | Epsom Salt |
|---|---|---|
| 20% Green Tea | 10% Gelatin | 1% Epsom Salt |
| 80% Water | 90% Water | 99% Water |

**20.** Complete the table to show the unit rates for the ingredients in the Gelatin Recipe.

| | | | |
|---|---|---|---|
| **Cups of Gelatin** | | | 1 |
| **Cups of Water** | | 1 | |
| **Total Cups in Mix** | 100 | | |

**21.** Write two equations relating the number of cups of gelatin *G* and the number of cups of water *W* in the gelatin plant food recipe.

**22. a.** Linda calculates that she uses 55 cups of mix to feed all of her plants. How many cups each of gelatin and water does she need to make enough mixture?

**b.** Describe two ways to solve part (a).

# Additional Practice (continued)

For Exercises 23–24, use the following information.

The table shows some recipes for organic plant foods.

| Green Tea Recipe | Gelatin (for Nitrogen) | Epsom Salt |
|---|---|---|
| 20% Green Tea | 10% Gelatin | 1% Epsom Salt |
| 80% Water | 90% Water | 99% Water |

23. Linda considers an experiment using a mixture of both green tea and gelatin with water as a monthly plant food. Find the unit rates for different mixtures. Consider the unit rate to be number of cups of green tea mixture per 1 cup of gelatin mixture.

   a. 50% green tea mix and 50% gelatin mix

   b. 40% green tea mix and 60% gelatin mix

   c. 75% green tea mix and 25% gelatin mix

   d. 80% green tea mix and 20% gelatin mix

24. For each unit rate of green tea mix and gelatin mix, calculate the percentage of plant food that is green tea mix and percentage of plant food that is gelatin mix.

   a. 1 cup green tea mix to 1 cup of gelatin mix

   b. 2 cups of green tea mix to 1 cup of gelatin mix

   c. 1 cup of green tea mix to 5 cups of gelatin mix

## Additional Practice (continued)

**For Exercise 25, use the following information.**

**The table shows some recipes for organic plant foods.**

| Green Tea Recipe | Gelatin (for Nitrogen) | Epsom Salt |
|---|---|---|
| 20% Green Tea | 10% Gelatin | 1% Epsom Salt |
| 80% Water | 90% Water | 99% Water |

**25.** Linda finds that the best results come from a mixture of 4 cups of gelatin mix and 60 cups of green tea mix.

   **a.** How many cups each of gelatin and water are in the 4 cups of gelatin mix?

   **b.** How many cups each of green tea and water are in the 60 cups of green tea mix?

   **c.** How many total cups of water are in the mix?

   **d.** What percentages of the total mixture are gelatin, green tea, and water?

# Additional Practice (continued)

**Use the following information for Exercises 26 and 27.**

**There are 16 left-handed students in Ms. Tatum's class. The other 20 students in her class are right-handed. Three students each computed the percentage of the class who were left-handed.**

**26.** Estimate the percentage of the class who are left-handed. Explain your reasoning.

**27.** Three students each computed the percentage of the class who were left-handed. Their explanations are shown below.

- **Andy:** I set up the proportion $\frac{16}{36} = \frac{\square}{100}$. Then I divided 16 by 36 and multiplied by 100. My answer was about 44%.

- **Mollie:** Since 20 is a factor of 100, I multiplied both 16 and 20 by 5 to get 80 and 100, respectively. A ratio of 80 left-handed students to 100 total students is 80%.

- **Natalie:** I noticed that both 16 and 20 were divisible by 4, which means the ratio of left-handed students to right-handed students is equivalent to $\frac{4}{5}$, and the ratio of left-handed students to the total students in the class is $\frac{4}{9}$ or $\frac{400}{900}$. So I divided 400 by 9 to get $44\frac{4}{9}$%.

  **a.** Which of the students' methods are correct? How do you know?

  **b.** Which of the students' methods make most sense to you? Explain.

# Additional Practice: Digital Assessments

**28.** A smoothie is made of 60% fruit and 40% water. If 4 cups of smoothie is to be made, which ingredient measures can be added to the smoothie mixture? *Select all that apply.*

☐ 2.4 cups of fruit

☐ 2.4 cups of water

☐ 1.6 cups of fruit

☐ 1.6 cups of water

☐ 1.5 cups of fruit

☐ 1.5 cups of water

**29.** A microwave cost $135. A coupon offers 15% off. Sales tax is 7%.

**a.** The amount of the discount with the coupon is $\begin{bmatrix} \$15.00 \\ \$20.25 \\ \$67.50 \\ \$114.75 \\ \$120.00 \end{bmatrix}$.

**b.** Without the coupon, the amount of tax would be $\begin{bmatrix} \$9.45 \\ \$20.25 \\ \$18.90 \\ \$94.50 \\ \$144.45 \end{bmatrix}$.

**30.** The rent for a retail store is $126 per square yard per year. Using only the number and symbols on the tiles provided below, fill in each space to write an expression that can be used to find the rent for one square foot per month.

# Skill: Proportional Relationships

Use each measurement conversion rate to complete the table. Write two equations representing the proportional relationship.

**1.** 1 yard = 3 feet

| Yards | 1 |   | 2 |   | 5 |
|-------|---|---|---|---|---|
| Feet  |   | 1 |   | 4 |   |

**2.** 1 centimeter = 10 millimeters

| Centimeters | 1 |   | 5 |    |    |
|-------------|---|---|---|----|----|
| Millimeters |   | 1 |   | 25 | 90 |

**3.** 1 week = 7 days

| Weeks | 1 |   | 4 |    |    |
|-------|---|---|---|----|----|
| Days  |   | 1 |   | 21 | 56 |

**4.** 1 gallon = 4 quarts

| Gallons | 1 |   | 2.5 |    | 11 |
|---------|---|---|-----|----|----|
| Quarts  |   | 1 |     | 36 |    |

**5.** 1 pound = 16 ounces

| Pounds | 1 |   | 3 |    | 12 |
|--------|---|---|---|----|----|
| Ounces |   | 1 |   | 88 |    |

**6.** 1 cup = 0.5 pint

| Cups  | 1 |   | 5 |    |    |
|-------|---|---|---|----|----|
| Pints |   | 1 |   | 25 | 90 |

# Skill: Proportional Relationships (continued)

**Determine if each table represents a proportional relationship. Explain how you know.**

**7.**

| °F | 32 | 77 | 122 | 167 | 212 |
|---|---|---|---|---|---|
| °C | 0 | 25 | 50 | 75 | 100 |

**8.**

| Miles | 0.25 | 0.5 | 1.0 | 2.0 | 4.0 |
|---|---|---|---|---|---|
| Dollars | 5 | 6 | 8 | 12 | 20 |

**9.**

| Pages | 1 | 2 | 3 | 10 | 20 |
|---|---|---|---|---|---|
| Dollars | 0.25 | 0.50 | 0.75 | 2.50 | 5.00 |

**10.**

| Words | 250 | 500 | 750 | 1,000 | 1,500 |
|---|---|---|---|---|---|
| Minutes | 5 | 10 | 15 | 20 | 30 |

Name _____ Date _____ Class _____

# Additional Practice

**For Exercises 1–2, refer to this table.**

| Cycling time (hours) | Distance (miles) | | |
|---|---|---|---|
| | Francine | Geraldo | Jennifer |
| 0 | 0 | 0 | 0 |
| 1 | 4.5 | 6 | 7.5 |
| 2 | 9 | 12 | 15 |
| 3 | 13.5 | 18 | 22.5 |
| 4 | 18 | 24 | 30 |

**1. a.** How fast was each person traveling? Explain.

**b.** Assume that each person continued at this rate. Find the distance each person traveled in 6 hours.

**2. a.** For each rider, write an equation you can use to calculate the distance traveled after a given number of hours.

**b.** Describe how you could use your equations to calculate the distance each person traveled in 2.5 hours.

**c.** How does each person's biking rate show up in the equation?

**d.** Are these examples of proportional or nonproportional relationships?

# Additional Practice (continued)

**For Exercise 3, refer to this table.**

| Cycling time (hours) | Distance (miles) | | |
|---|---|---|---|
| | Francine | Geraldo | Jennifer |
| 0 | 0 | 0 | 0 |
| 1 | 4.5 | 6 | 7.5 |
| 2 | 9 | 12 | 15 |
| 3 | 13.5 | 18 | 22.5 |
| 4 | 18 | 24 | 30 |

**3. a.** Graph the time and distance for all three people on the same coordinate axes.

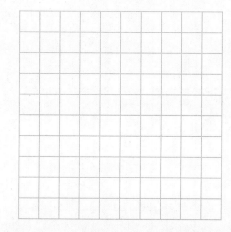

**b.** Use the graphs to find the distance each person traveled in 2.5 hours.

**c.** Use the graphs to find the time it took each person to travel 70 miles.

**d.** How does the rate at which each person rides affect the graphs?

**4.** Stilton was also on the bike trip. The distance he traveled after $t$ hours is represented by $d = 7.25t$.

**a.** At what rate of speed is Stilton traveling?

**b.** If you graphed Stilton's distance and time on the same set of axes as the graphs for the bike riders in Exercise 3, how would it compare to the other three graphs?

## Additional Practice (continued)

**5.** Martin used some rules to generate the following tables:

i.

| x | y |
|----|----|
| −1 | 6 |
| 0 | 8 |
| 1 | 10 |
| 2 | 12 |
| 3 | 14 |

ii.

| x | y |
|----|----|
| 0 | 5 |
| 3 | 5 |
| 6 | 5 |
| 9 | 5 |
| 12 | 5 |

iii.

| x | y |
|----|------|
| −2 | −5 |
| −1 | −4.5 |
| 0 | −4 |
| 3 | −2.5 |
| 4 | −2 |
| 5 | −1.5 |

iv.

| x | y |
|----|------|
| −1 | 0.5 |
| 0 | 0 |
| 1 | 0.5 |
| 2 | 2 |
| 3 | 4.5 |
| 4 | 8 |
| 5 | 12.5 |

**a.** Make a graph of the data in each table. Show the graphs on the same coordinate axes.

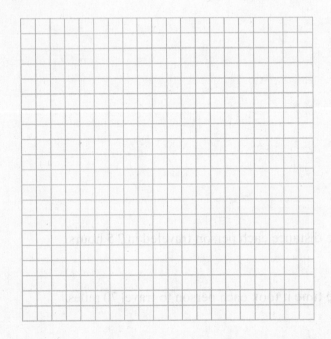

**b.** Which sets of data represent a linear relationship? How do you know?

**c.** Do any sets of data represent proportional relationships? Explain.

# Additional Practice: Digital Assessments

**6.** A car travels at a constant speed so that every minute it travels 1.4 km. Circle the number or phrase that makes each statement true.

   **a.** The distance traveled in 40 minutes is

$$\begin{bmatrix} 41 \\ 43 \\ 54 \\ 56 \\ 64 \end{bmatrix} \text{km.}$$

   **b.** It takes the car $\begin{bmatrix} 14 \\ 15 \\ 20 \\ 22.4 \\ 29.4 \end{bmatrix}$ minutes to travel 21 kilometers.

   **c.** This situation $\begin{bmatrix} \text{does} \\ \text{does not} \end{bmatrix}$ represent a proportional relationship.

**7.** Brenna saves $7 per week.

   **a.** Which equation represents the relationship between Brenna's total savings, *B*, and time, *w*?

     ○ $B = \frac{1}{7} w$

     ○ $B = 7w$

     ○ $B = -7w$

     ○ $7B = w$

   **b.** Which are descriptions of the graph that models the situation? *Select all that apply.*

     ☐ The graph is a line.

     ☐ The graph has a *y*-intercept of 7.

     ☐ The graph passes through the origin.

     ☐ The graph is increasing.

     ☐ The graph intersects the point (21, 3).

**8.** Apples are on sale for $0.75 per apple. Using the numbers on the tiles provided, fill in each space in the table to model the relationship between cost and number of apples purchased.

| Number of Apples | Cost |
|---|---|
|  | $1.50 |
| 4 | $ |
| 12 | $ |
|  | $3.75 |

| | | |
|---|---|---|
| 2 | 3 | 5 |
| 7 | 9 | 10 |

# Skill: Linear Relationships

1. You order books through a catalog. Each book costs $12 and the shipping and handling cost is $5. Write an equation and make a graph that represents your total cost.

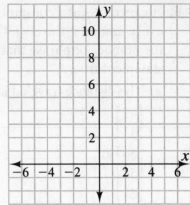

 a. What is the total cost if you buy 6 books?

 b. What is the total cost if you buy 4 books?

2. A ride in a taxicab costs $2.50 for the first mile and $1.50 for each additional mile or part of a mile. Write an equation and make a graph that represents the total cost.

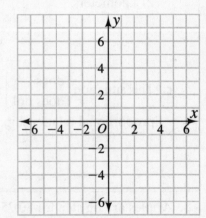

 a. What is the total cost of a 10-mile ride?

 b. What is the total cost of a 25-mile ride?

# Skill: Linear Relationships (continued)

**3.** A tree is 3 feet tall and grows 3 inches each day.
Write an equation and make a graph that represents
how much the tree grows over time.

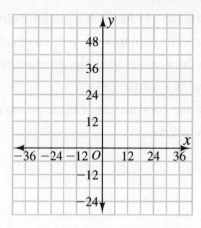

 

**a.** How tall is the tree in a week?

 

**b.** How tall is the tree in 4 weeks?

# Additional Practice

**1.** Do parts (a)–(e) for each equation below.

    **a.** Graph the equation on your calculator, and make a sketch of the line you see.

    **b.** Do the $y$-values increase, decrease, or stay the same as the $x$-values increase?

    **c.** Give the $y$-intercept.

    **d.** List the coordinates of three points on the line.

      **i.** $y = 2.5x$

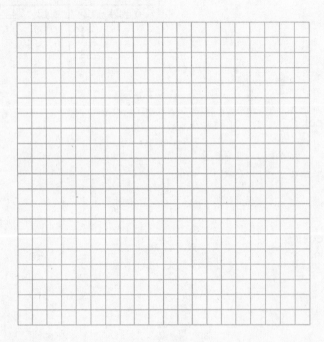

      **ii.** $y = -2x + 7$

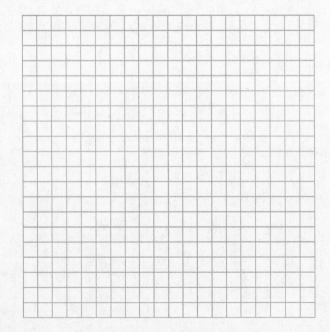

# Additional Practice (continued)

**1.** Do parts (a)–(e) for each equation below.

   **a.** Graph the equation on your calculator, and make a sketch of the line you see.

   **b.** Do the *y*-values increase, decrease, or stay the same as the *x*-values increase?

   **c.** Give the *y*-intercept.

   **d.** List the coordinates of three points on the line.

    **iii.** $y = -4x - 8$

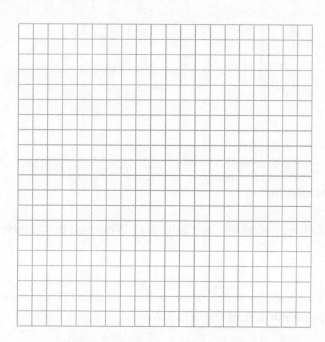

    **iv.** $y = 3x - 3$

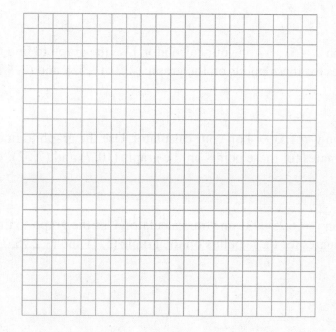

# Additional Practice (continued)

**2.** The volleyball team decided to raise money for an end-of-season party by selling school buttons. The costs and the revenue of selling the buttons are shown on the graph below.

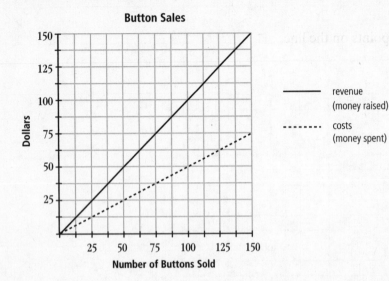

**Button Sales**

**a.** If the team sells 50 buttons, what will be their cost? What will be the revenue?

**b.** If the team sells 50 buttons, how much profit will they make? (Remember that the profit is the revenue minus the cost.)

**c.** If the team sells 100 buttons, how much profit will they make?

**3. a.** Graph the equation $y = 5x + 7$ on your calculator. Use the graph to find the missing coordinates for these points on the graph: $(2, ?), (?, 52)$, and $(2.9, ?)$.

**b.** Graph the equation $y = 1.5x - 4$ on your calculator. Use the graph to find the missing coordinates for these points on the graph: $(10, ?)$ and $(?, 32)$.

**c.** Graph the equation $y = 6.25 - 3x$ on your calculator. Use the graph to find the missing coordinates for these points on the graph: $(5, ?)$ and $(-2.75, ?)$.

# Additional Practice (continued)

**4.** Use the graph at the right to answer parts (a)–(d).

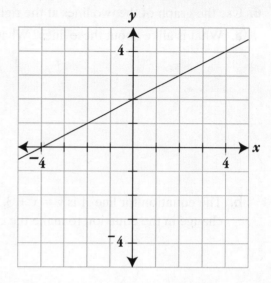

  **a.** List the coordinates of three points on the line.

  **b.** Which equation below is the equation of the line?

   **i.** $y = x + 4$      **ii.** $y = 0.5x + 2$

   **iii.** $y = 0.5x - 5$   **iv.** $y = 4 - 0.5x$

  **c.** Does the point $(56, 35)$ lie on the line? Explain.

  **d.** Does the point $(-20, -8)$ lie on the line? Explain.

**5.** Use the graph of the three lines to complete the table.

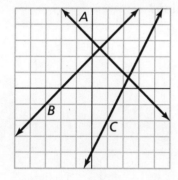

| Line | Constant Rate of Change | y-intercept | x-intercept |
|------|------------------------|-------------|-------------|
| A    |                        |             |             |
| B    |                        |             |             |
| C    |                        |             |             |

  **b.** Match each line on the graph with one of these equations:

   $y = 2 + x$,    $y = -4 + 2x$,    $y = 3 - x$

   line $A$: _____,  line $B$: _____,  line $C$: _____

# Additional Practice (continued)

**6.** Use the graph of the two lines at the right.

    **a.** What is alike about these lines? What is different?

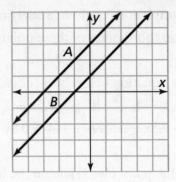

    **b.** The equation for line $A$ is $y = x + 3$. What do you think would have to change in the equation to make the equation for line $B$? Explain.

    **c.** Write the equation for line $B$.

    **d.** Imagine a line halfway between lines $A$ and $B$. What is its equation? Explain.

    **e.** Do any of these lines represent a proportional relationship?

**7. a.** Use the graph below to complete the table.

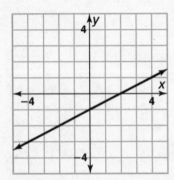

| $x$ | −3 | 0 | 2 | 5 | 7 | 10 | 100 |
|---|---|---|---|---|---|---|---|
| $y$ | | | | | | | |

    **b.** Explain your reasoning for the last three $y$-values.

# Additional Practice (continued)

**8. a.** For each pair of lines, find the point of intersection.

$y = x$  and  $y = -x$

$y = x + 1$  and  $y = -x + 1$

$y = x + 3$  and  $y = -x + 3$

$y = x - 4$  and  $y = -x - 4$

**b.** What pattern do you see?

**c.** Without graphing the lines, where is the point of intersection of these lines?

$y = x + 137$  and  $y = -x + 137$

## Additional Practice (continued)

**For Exercises 9–11, use the graph at the right.**

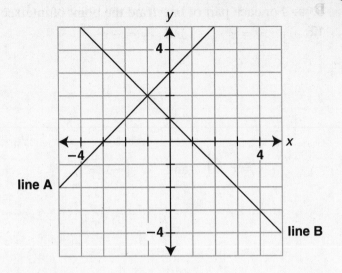

9. Make a table showing the coordinates of four points located on line A. What is the equation for line A?

10. Make a table showing the coordinates of four points located on line B. What is the equation for line B?

11. Is there a point with $(x, y)$ coordinates that satisfies both the equation for line A and the equation for line B? Explain your reasoning.

## Additional Practice (continued)

**Does the point represent a point on the graph of $y = x - 4$?**

**12.** $(0, -4)$       **13.** $(5, -1)$       **14.** $(-3, -7)$       **15.** $(-7, -3)$

**16.** Each set of $(x, y)$ coordinates below is generated by a linear rule. For each set of coordinates, write an equation to describe the rule.

   **a.** $(-1, -7), (0, -3), (1, 1), (2, 5), (4, 13), (5, 17)$

   **b.** $(-2, 19), (-1, 14), (0, 9), (2, -1), (4, -11), (6, -21)$

   **c.** $(-2, -1), (0, 3), (1, 5), (3, 9), (5, 13), (6, 15)$

**Write an equation for each graph.**

**17.**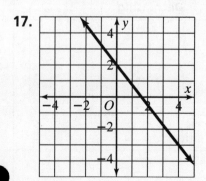

**18.**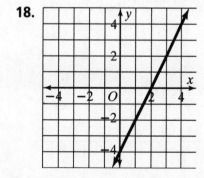

# Additional Practice: Digital Assessments

**19.** Circle the number that makes the ordered pair a solution of the equation $y = 5 - 2x$.

**a.** $\left(-1, \begin{bmatrix} -5 \\ -1 \\ 1 \\ 6 \\ 7 \end{bmatrix}\right)$

**b.** $\left(\begin{bmatrix} -3 \\ -1 \\ 0 \\ 2 \\ 5 \end{bmatrix}, 1\right)$

**20.** Which equation represents the equation of the line? *Select all that apply.*

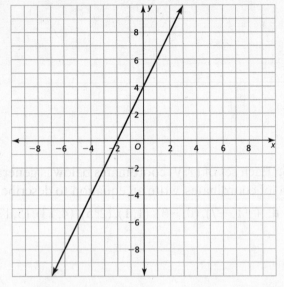

☐ $y = 2 + x$

☐ $y = x + 2$

☐ $y = 2x + 4$

☐ $y = 2x - 4$

☐ $y = 4 + 2x$

☐ $y = 4x - 2$

**21.** Write each equation in the box with the correct category.

$y = \frac{1}{2}x + 3$    $y = 6 - x$    $y = -3x + 14$    $y = \frac{1}{4}x - 5$    $y = 5x$    $y = 5 + x$

| Increasing | Decreasing |
|---|---|
|  |  |

# Skill: Linear Functions, Graphs, and Tables

1. A ride in a cab costs $0.60 plus $0.14 per mile.

   a. Write an equation for traveling $x$ miles in the cab.

   b. The cab charges $0.88 for a ride of how many miles?

   c. How much does the cab charge for a trip of 8 miles?

**Graph each linear equation.**

2. $y = -4x + 6$

3. $y = -2x + 7$

4. $y = -3x - 1$

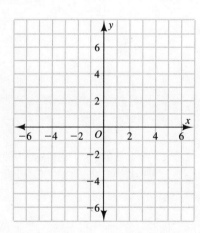 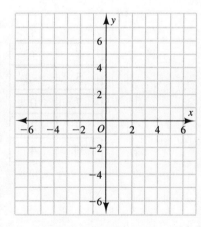 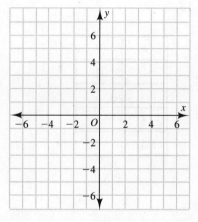

Name _____ Date _____ Class _____

# Skill: Linear Functions, Graphs, and Tables (continued)

On which of the following lines does each point lie? A point may lie on more than one line.

$\quad\quad$ **A.** $y = x + 5$ $\quad\quad$ **B.** $y = -x + 7$ $\quad\quad$ **C.** $y = 2x - 1$

**5.** $(0, 5)$ $\quad\quad\quad$ **6.** $(1, 6)$ $\quad\quad\quad$ **7.** $\frac{8}{3}, \frac{13}{3}$ $\quad\quad\quad$ **8.** $(0, -1)$

**9.** $(4, 9)$ $\quad\quad\quad$ **10.** $(4, 3)$ $\quad\quad\quad$ **11.** $(-2, -5)$ $\quad\quad\quad$ **12.** $(-8, 15)$

Decide if each table represents a linear relationship. For those that do, write an equation that represents the relationship.

**13.**

| $x$ | $y$ |
|---|---|
| −3 | 18 |
| −1 | 6 |
| 1 | −6 |
| 3 | −18 |

**14.**

| $x$ | $y$ |
|---|---|
| 5 | −2 |
| 7 | 0 |
| 9 | 2 |
| 11 | 4 |

**15.**

| $x$ | $y$ |
|---|---|
| −3 | −17 |
| −1 | −11 |
| 1 | −5 |
| 3 | 1 |

**16.**

| $x$ | $y$ |
|---|---|
| −4 | 4 |
| 0 | 6 |
| 2 | 7 |
| 4 | 8 |

# Additional Practice

1. The equations below represent the costs to print brochures at three printers.

   **a.** For which equation does the point $(20, 60)$ lie on the graph? Explain.

   **i.** $C = 15 + 2.50N$     **ii.** $C = 50 + 1.75N$     **iii.** $C = 30 + 1.50N$

   **b.** For each equation, give the coordinates of one point on the graph of the equation.

2. The equations below represent the distances in meters traveled after $t$ seconds by three cyclists.

   **a.** For which equation does the point $(10, 74)$ lie on the graph? Explain.

   **i.** $D = 2.4t + 32$     **ii.** $D = 4.2t + 32$     **iii.** $D = 6t + 32$

   **b.** For each equation, give the coordinates of a point on the graph of the equation.

3. Do parts (a) and (b) for each pair of equations below.

   **i.** $y = -\frac{12}{5}x - 6$        **ii.** $y = x - 3$
   $y = 4x + 14$             $y = -1.5x + 12$

   **iii.** $y = x + 9$         **iv.** $y = 2x - 6$
   $y = 7 - 3x$            $y = -2$

   **a.** Using your calculator, graph the two equations on the same axes. Use window settings that allow you to see the points where the graphs intersect. What ranges of $x$- and $y$-values did you use for your window?

   **b.** Find the point of intersection of the graphs. Then test each point of intersection you found by substituting its coordinates into the equations. Did the points fit the equation exactly? Explain why or why not.

# Additional Practice (continued)

**4. a.** Find $r$ if $2r + 10 = 22$.

**b.** Find $x$ if $4.5x = 45$.

**c.** Find $z$ if $3z - 19 = 173$.

**d.** Find $w$ if $67.1 = 29.7 - 0.2w$.

**5.** Betty is thinking of two consecutive integers whose sum is 41. Let $x$ represent the smaller unknown integer.

**a.** How could you represent the larger unknown integer in terms of $x$?

**b.** Write and solve an equation showing that the sum of the two unknown integers is 41. What integers is Betty thinking of?

**6.** Find the number described in each problem by writing and solving an equation.

**a.** If Sarah subtracts five times her number from 24, she gets 4. What is Sarah's number?

**b.** Twice Bill's number added to 17 is 7. What is Bill's number?

**c.** If Susan subtracts 11 from one fourth of her number, she gets 11. What is Susan's number?

## Additional Practice (continued)

7. The school drama club is performing a play at the community theater. Props cost $250, and the theater is charging the drama club $1.25 for each ticket sold. So, the total cost $C$ for the drama club to put on the play is $C = 1.25N + 250$, where $N$ is the number of tickets sold. Customers pay $4 for each ticket, so the total amount collected from ticket sales is $T = 4N$.

a. What is the cost if 213 tickets are sold?

b. How much are the total ticket sales if 213 tickets are sold?

c. What is the drama club's profit or loss if 213 tickets are sold?

d. If the total ticket sales are $780, how many people attended the play?

e. What is the cost of putting on the play for the number of people you found in part (d)?

f. How many tickets does the drama club need to sell to break even?

g. The drama club would like to earn a profit of $500 from the play. How many tickets need to be sold for the club to meet this goal?

# Additional Practice *(continued)*

8. In each pair of equations, solve the first equation and graph the second equation:

   **a.** $0 = 3x + 6$ $\qquad$ $y = 3x + 6$

   **b.** $0 = x - 2$ $\qquad$ $y = x - 2$

   **c.** $0 = 3x + 10$ $\qquad$ $y = 3x + 10$

   **d.** In each pair, how is the solution to the first equation related to the graph?

## Additional Practice (continued)

**9.** Marsha said there are two ways to solve the equation $3x + 15 = 24$.

| | | | |
|---|---|---|---|
| $3x + 15 = 24$ | Subtract 15 from each side. | $3x + 15 = 24$ | Divide each side by 3. |
| $3x = 9$ | Divide each side by 3. | $x + 5 = 8$ | Subtract 5 from each side. |
| $x = 3$ | | $x = 3$ | |

**a.** Are both strategies correct? Explain.

**b.** Which strategy do you think is easier? Explain.

**c.** How do you know when you can divide first?

**d.** Solve this equation in two ways: $5x + 20 = 5$.

**10.** Find $x$ if
   **a.** $x + 7 = 20$      **b.** $3x + 7 = 20$      **c.** $-2x + 7 = 20$

   **d.** How are the solutions similar? How are they different?

# Additional Practice (continued)

**11.** If $y = \frac{2}{3}x + 4$, find $y$ if

**a.** $x = 0$  **b.** $x = 3$  **c.** $x = 9$

**d.** $x = -9$  **e.** $x = 10$  **f.** $x = \frac{1}{2}$

**12.** Kelli is having a graduation party and needs to stay within a budget of \$1,250 for the food. One caterer charges \$13.50 per person, $p$. A second caterer charges \$100 to set up, and then \$12.00 per person.

**a.** Write an inequality to show the number of people that can attend if Kelli stays within her budget and uses the first caterer.

**b.** Write an inequality to show the number of people that can attend if Kelli stays within her budget and uses the second caterer.

**c.** For each inequality:

**i.** find the number of people who can attend if Kelli stays within her budget. Remember to round your solution to the nearest whole value that makes sense in the context.

**ii.** record the solution on a number line.

**d.** Which caterer would you choose? Explain why.

# Additional Practice: Digital Assessments

**13.** Entry into a theme park costs $25. Inside the theme park, there is an arcade where each game is $0.50. Which equations relate the cost, $C$, of going to the theme park to the number of games played, $g$? *Select all that apply.*

☐ $C = 25 + 0.5g$

☐ $C = 0.5 + 25g$

☐ $C = 0.5g + 25$

☐ $C = 25 - 0.5g$

☐ $C = -25 + 0.5g$

☐ $C = -25 - 0.5g$

**14.** Circle the coordinates of the point that is a solution to both equations.

$$y = 4 - 3x$$

$$y = \frac{1}{2}x - 3$$

$$\left( \begin{bmatrix} -2 \\ 1 \\ 2 \\ 4 \\ 6 \end{bmatrix}, \begin{bmatrix} -3 \\ -2 \\ 0 \\ 1 \\ 10 \end{bmatrix} \right)$$

**15.** Write each equation in the box with the correct solution.

$$-3 = 2x + 3 \qquad 3 = 6 - x \qquad 5 = -3x + 14 \qquad -6 = \frac{1}{3}x - 5 \qquad 6 = -2x \qquad 2 = 5 + x$$

| $x = 3$ |
|---|
|  |

| $x = -3$ |
|---|
|  |

# Skill: Exploring Equality

1. Determine whether each point is a solution of $y = 3x - 8$.

   **a.** $(0, -8)$    **b.** $(6, -10)$    **c.** $(-2, -2)$    **d.** $(4, 4)$

2. Determine whether each point is a solution of $y = -5x + 19$.

   **a.** $(-3, 4)$    **b.** $(0, 19)$    **c.** $(2, 9)$    **d.** $(-4, 39)$

**Use the equation $y = -2x + 1$. Complete each solution.**

3. $(0, \Box)$    4. $(-5, \Box)$    5. $(20, \Box)$    6. $(-68, \Box)$

**Use each equation. Find $y$ for $x = 1, 2, 3,$ and $4$.**

7. $y = 2x$    8. $y = 3x + 1$

9. $y = x - 5$    10. $y = -5x + 6$

# Skill: Finding the Point of Intersection

**Will these lines intersect? Explain.**

**1.** $y = 6x + 12$
$y = 2x - 4$

**2.** $y = -3x$
$y = \frac{1}{4}x - \frac{1}{8}$

**3.** $y = -\frac{1}{2}x + 1$
$y = -\frac{2}{5}x + \frac{2}{5}$

**4.** Find the point of intersection of the two lines by graphing.

$y = -x + 3$
$y = x + 1$

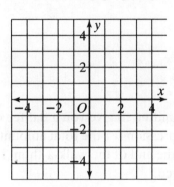

**5.** Tomatoes are $0.80 per pound at Rob's Market, and $1.20 per pound at Sal's Produce. You have a coupon for $1.40 off at Sal's. (Assume that you buy at least $1.40 worth of tomatoes.)

   **a.** Write an equation relating the cost $y$ to the number of pounds $x$ at each market.

   Rob's: _____ Sal's: _____

   **b.** Use a graph to estimate the number of pounds for which the cost is the same at either store.

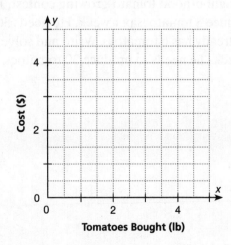

# Skill: Solving Linear Equations

**Solve each equation. Check your answers.**

**1.** $10 + 5h = 25$

**2.** $8s - 8 = 64$

**3.** $3y + 78 = 81$

**4.** $2g + 4 = 12$

**5.** $5j + 5 = 15$

**6.** $3w + 8 = 20$

**7.** For a walk-a-thon, a sponsor committed to give you a flat fee of $5 plus $2 for every mile you walk. Write an expression for the total amount of money you will collect from your sponsor at the end of the walk-a-thon. Then evaluate your expression for 20 miles walked.

**8.** To win the neighborhood tomato-growing contest, Johnny needs his tomato plants to produce 8 tomatoes per week. He needs 30 tomatoes to win the contest. He already has 6 tomatoes. Write and solve an equation to find the number of weeks he needs to produce 30 tomatoes.

# Skill: Solving Linear Equations (continued)

**For Exercises 9–14, solve each equation.**

**9.** $4r + 6 = 14$   **10.** $9y - 11 = 7$   **11.** $-5b - 6 = -11$

**12.** $-9i - 17 = -26$   **13.** $14.9 = 8.6 + 0.9m$   **14.** $15w - 21 = -111$

**15.** Hugo received $100 for his birthday. He then saved $20 per week until he had a total of $460 to buy a printer. Use an equation to show how many weeks it took him to save the money.

**16.** A health club charges a $50 initial fee plus $2 for each visit. Moselle has spent a total of $144 at the health club this year. Use an equation to find how many visits she has made.

# Additional Practice

1. Find the slope and *y*-intercept of the line represented by each equation.

   **a.** $y = 2x - 10$     **b.** $y = 4x + 3$     **c.** $y = 4x - 4.5$

   **d.** $y = 2.6x$     **e.** $y = 7x + 1$

2. Each table in (i.)–(v.) below represents a linear relationship. Do parts (a)–(c) for each table.

   **a.** Find the slope of the line that represents the relationship.

   **b.** Find the *y*-intercept for the graph of the relationship.

   **c.** Determine which of the following equations represents the relationship:

   $y = 3 - 4x$     $y = x + 6$     $y = 4x - 3$     $y = 3x - 1.5$     $y = 2.5x$

**i.**

| x | y |
|---|---|
| 0 | 0 |
| 1 | 2.5 |
| 2 | 5 |
| 3 | 7.5 |
| 4 | 10 |

**ii.**

| x | y |
|---|---|
| 0 | 6 |
| 1 | 7 |
| 2 | 8 |
| 3 | 9 |
| 4 | 10 |

**iii.**

| x | y |
|---|---|
| 0 | −1.5 |
| 1 | 1.5 |
| 2 | 4.5 |
| 3 | 7.5 |
| 4 | 10.5 |

**iv.**

| x | y |
|---|---|
| 1 | −1 |
| 2 | −5 |
| 3 | −9 |
| 4 | −13 |

**v.**

| x | y |
|---|---|
| 1 | 5 |
| 2 | 9 |
| 3 | 13 |
| 4 | 17 |

# Additional Practice *(continued)*

**3.** For each of the lines below, find the slope and write an equation that represents the line.

**a.**

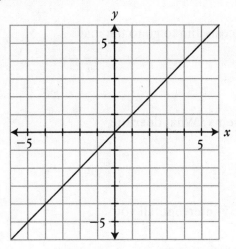

**b.**

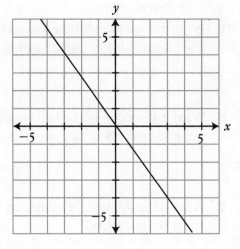

**c.**

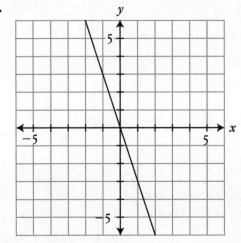

**4.** Do parts (a)–(d) for each pair of points below.

  **a.** Plot the points on a coordinate grid, and draw the line through the points.

  **b.** Find the slope of the line through the points.

  **c.** Estimate the *y*-intercept from the graph.

  **d.** Using your answers from parts (a) and (b), write an equation for the line through the points.

    **i.** $(0, 0)$ and $(-3, -3)$          **ii.** $(1, -1)$ and $(-3, 3)$

# **Additional Practice** (continued)

**5.** On Saturdays, Jim likes to go to the mall to play video games or pinball. Round-trip bus fare to and from the mall is $1.80. Jim spends $0.50 for each video or pinball game.

   **a.** Write an equation for the amount of money $M$ it costs Jim to go to the mall and play $n$ video or pinball games.

   **b.** What is the slope of the line your equation represents? What does the slope tell you about this situation?

   **c.** What is the $y$-intercept of the line? What does the $y$-intercept tell you about the situation?

   **d.** How much will it cost Jim to travel to the mall and play 8 video or pinball games?

   **e.** If Jim has $6.75, how many video or pinball games can he play at the mall?

**6.** The graph below shows the total cost (including bus fare and the cost of comics) for Angie to go to the Comic Shop to buy new comic books.

   **a.** What is Angie's round-trip bus fare? Explain your reasoning.

   **b.** How much does a comic book cost at the Comic Shop? Explain.

   **c.** Write an equation that shows how much money $M$ it costs Angie to buy $n$ comic books at the Comic Shop. What information did you use from the graph to write the equation? Is this a proportional relationship?

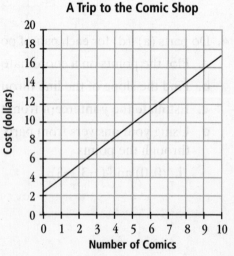

A Trip to the Comic Shop

## Additional Practice (continued)

7. Tonya is siphoning all the water from a full aquarium to clean it. The graph at the right shows the amount of water left in the aquarium as Tonya siphons the water.

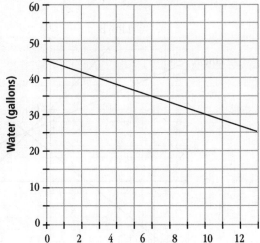

Siphoning an Aquarium

a. How much water was in the aquarium when it was full? Explain.

b. How much water does the siphon remove from the aquarium in 1 minute? Explain.

c. Write an equation that shows the amount of water *G* left in the aquarium after *t* minutes.

d. How many gallons of water are left in the aquarium after 10 minutes?

e. How long will it take the siphon to remove all of the water from the aquarium? Explain.

8. For parts (a)–(e), write an equation for the line that satisfies the given conditions.

a. The slope is 7 and the *y*-intercept is $-2$.

b. The slope is 0 and the *y*-intercept is 9.18.

c. The line passes through the points $(-24, -11)$ and $(-8, -3)$.

d. The line passes through the points $(-4.5, 2)$ and $(6.3, 5.8)$.

e. The slope is $-\frac{2}{3}$, and the line passes through the point $(5, 0)$.

9. Write an equation for each of the four lines shown on the graph below.

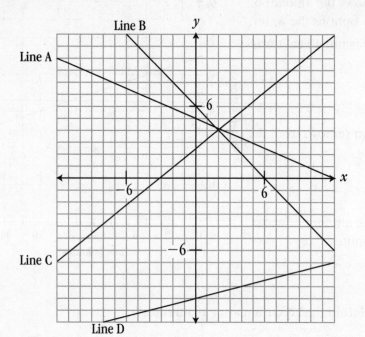

10. At Midtown Bowling Center, the cost to bowl four games is $8.40, and the cost to rent shoes is $1.15.

   **a.** Write an equation for the cost $C$ for renting shoes and bowling $n$ games.

   **b.** What is the $y$-intercept for your equation, and what does it represent?

   **c.** What is the slope of your equation, and what does the slope represent?

   **d.** What is the cost of renting shoes and bowling 6 games?

   **e.** Tony paid $7.45 for his games and shoe rental. How many games did Tony bowl?

# Additional Practice (continued)

**11.** Here are some possible descriptions of a line:

| Slope | *y*-intercept | *x*-axis |
|---|---|---|
| positive | positive | passes through the origin $(0, 0)$ |
| equals 0 | equals 0 | crosses the *x*-axis to the right of the origin |
| negative | negative | crosses the *x*-axis to the left of the origin |
| | | never crosses the *x*-axis |

Use the descriptions above to describe the properties of the slope,
*y*-intercept, and *x*-axis for the graph of each equation.

**a.** $y = x$

**b.** $y = 2x + 1$

**c.** $y = -5$

**d.** $y = 4 - 3x$

**e.** $y = -3 - x$

**12.** These two points determine a line: $(-2, 10)$ and $(1, 4)$. Which of these points
is also on that line?

$(2, 0)$          $(2, 2)$          $(2, 10)$

# Additional Practice (continued)

**13.** Below are four patterns:

Pattern 1:

Figure 1          Figure 2          Figure 3

Pattern 2:

Figure 1          Figure 2          Figure 3

Pattern 3:

Figure 1          Figure 2          Figure 3

Pattern 4:

Figure 1          Figure 2          Figure 3

**a.** In each cell in the chart below, write the perimeter of the figure:

| Shape | Figure 1 | Figure 2 | Figure 3 | Figure 4 | Figure 10 | Figure 100 |
|-------|----------|----------|----------|----------|-----------|------------|
| Pattern 1 |  |  |  |  |  |  |
| Pattern 2 |  |  |  |  |  |  |
| Pattern 3 |  |  |  |  |  |  |
| Pattern 4 |  |  |  |  |  |  |

**b.** Describe the pattern of change within each pattern.

**c.** Explain how you found the values for the last three columns.

**d.** Write an equation for the perimeter of the figures for each pattern.

**14.** Line A is the graph of this equation: $y = 2x + 2$.
Line B is the graph of this equation: $y = 2x$.

   **a.** What is alike about lines A and B? What is different?

   **b.** Write the equation of a line that lies between line A and line B. How is your equation similar to the equations above? How is it different?

   **c.** Explain why your equation is correct.

# Additional Practice: Digital Assessments

**15.** Which are interpretations of the slope of the equation $y = 2x - 1$? *Select all that apply.*

☐ As $x$ increases by 2, $y$ increases by 1.

☐ As $x$ decreases by 2, $y$ increases by 1.

☐ As $x$ decreases by 2, $y$ decreases by 1.

☐ As $x$ increases by 1, $y$ increases by 2.

☐ As $x$ decreases by 1, $y$ increases by 2.

☐ As $x$ decreases by 1, $y$ decreases by 2.

**16.** Circle the numbers that complete the equation of the line with a slope of 3 and a $y$-intercept of 5.

$$y = \begin{bmatrix} -5 \\ -3 \\ 3 \\ 5 \end{bmatrix} x + \begin{bmatrix} -5 \\ -3 \\ 3 \\ 5 \end{bmatrix}$$

**17.** Circle the numbers that complete the equation of the line that passes through the points $(1, -1)$ and $(-2, 0)$.

$$y = \begin{bmatrix} -\frac{1}{3} \\ -3 \\ -1 \\ 1 \\ 3 \end{bmatrix} x + \begin{bmatrix} -2 \\ -\frac{2}{3} \\ -\frac{1}{3} \\ 0 \\ \frac{2}{3} \end{bmatrix}$$

**18.** Write each equation in the box with the correct category. Some equations may fit in more than one category.

$$y = 3x \qquad y = -2x + 5 \qquad y = \frac{1}{2}x - 1 \qquad y = 1 - x \qquad y = -x \qquad y = 2 - 3x$$

| Positive Slope | Passes Through the Origin | Positive $y$-intercept |
|---|---|---|
| | | |

# Skill: Finding Slope

**Find the slope of each line.**

1.

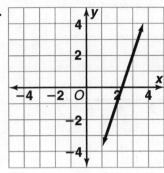

2.

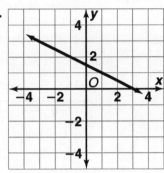

3.

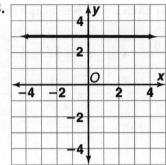

4.

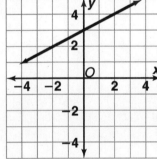

5.

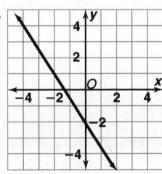

Name _____ Date _____ Class _____

# Skill: Finding Slope (continued)

**For Exercises 6–7, the points from each table lie on a line. Use the table to find the slope of each line. Then graph the line.**

**6.**

| x | 0 | 1 | 2 | 3 | 4 |
|---|---|---|---|---|---|
| y | −3 | −1 | 1 | 3 | 5 |

slope =

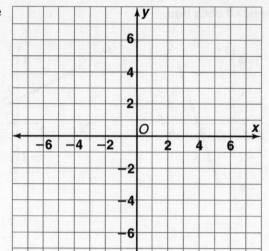

**7.**

| x | 0 | 1 | 2 | 3 | 4 |
|---|---|---|---|---|---|
| y | 5 | 3 | 1 | −1 | −3 |

slope =

**Find the slope of the line that passes through each pair of points.**

**8.** $A(1, 1), B(6, 3)$

**9.** $J(-4, 6), K(-4, 2)$

**10.** $P(3, -7), Q(-1, -7)$

**11.** $M(7, 2), N(-1, 3)$

# Skill: Using Slope

**For Exercises 1–4, determine if the line that represents each equation has the same slope as the equation $y = 2x - 4$.**

**1.** $y = 2x + 4$      **2.** $y = -2x + 3$      **3.** $y = 4x - 2$      **4.** $y = 3x - 4$

**5.** Which hill would it be easiest to push a heavy cart up: one with a slope of $\frac{1}{2}$, $\frac{1}{6}$, 3, or 5? Explain.

**6.** Which ski run would probably give you the greatest speed down a hill when you are skiing: one with a slope of $\frac{1}{8}$, $\frac{1}{4}$, 1, or 2?

**7.** Which roof would be the most dangerous for a roofer: one with a slope of $\frac{1}{16}$, $\frac{1}{10}$, $\frac{1}{2}$, or $\frac{3}{2}$?

**8.** Which of the slopes from Exercise 7 would be the easiest for the roofer?

**Draw a line with the given slope through the given point.**

**9.** $P(5, 1)$, slope $= -\frac{1}{3}$              **10.** $K(-2, 4)$, slope $= 3$

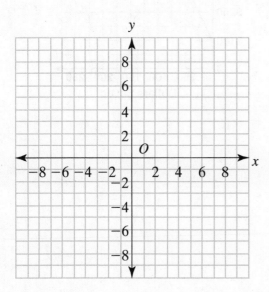 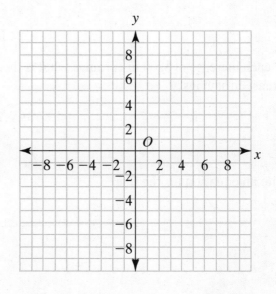

Name _____ Date _____ Class _____

# Skill: Writing Equations

**Moving Straight Ahead**

**Write an equation for each line.**

1.
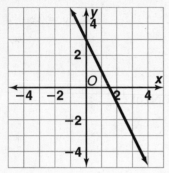

2.
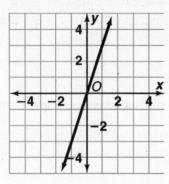

3.
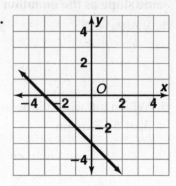

**Use the graph at the right for Exercises 4–8.**

4. What earnings will produce $225 in savings?

5. How much is saved from earnings of $400?

6. What is the slope of the line in the graph?

7. For each increase of $200 in earnings, what is the increase in savings?

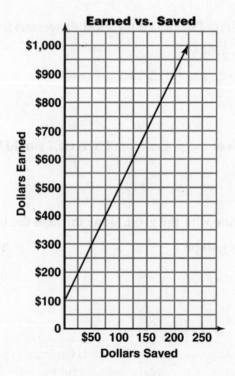

8. Write an equation for the line.

# Additional Practice

1. Students at Euler Middle School are talking about ways to raise money for a school party. One student suggests a game called *Heads or Tails*. In this game, a player pays 50 cents and chooses heads or tails. The player then tosses a fair coin. If the coin matches the player's call, the player wins a prize.

   **a.** Suppose 100 players play the game. How many of these players would you expect to win?

   **b.** Suppose the prizes awarded to winners of *Heads or Tails* cost 40 cents each. Based on your answer to part (a), how much money would you expect the students to raise if 100 players play the game? Explain.

   **c.** Do you think *Heads or Tails* is an effective game for raising money for the school party? Explain your reasoning.

2. Suppose you toss a fair coin 75 times.

   **a.** How many times would you expect to get heads?

   **b.** How many times would you expect to get tails?

   **c.** Juan tossed a coin 75 times. The coin landed heads up 50 times and tails up 25 times. Can you conclude that the coin is not a fair coin? Explain.

# Additional Practice (continued)

3. Joyce tossed a coin 10 times and recorded an "H" for each head and a "T" for each tail. Her results were: H, H, H, H, H, T, T, T, T, T.

   a. If you tossed a fair coin 10 times, would you expect to get the same number of heads and tails in the same order that Joyce got? Explain.

   b. Based on the results of Joyce's flips, do you think her coin is fair or not fair? Explain your reasoning.

4. Betty empties her piggy bank, which contains 210 coins, onto her desk.

   a. How many of the coins would you expect to be heads up?

   b. How many of the coins would you expect to be tails up?

5. If you toss one coin four times in a row, which is more likely:

   a. getting 2 heads and 2 tails or getting 3 heads and 1 tail? Explain.

   b. tossing HTHT, THTH, or HHTT? Explain.

# Additional Practice *(continued)*

**6.** Decide whether the possible results are equally likely. Explain.

| **Action** | **Result** |
|---|---|
| **a.** You pick a wildflower from a field. | The flower is a daisy, the flower is a buttercup, the flower is an aster, or the flower is a clover. |

**b.** You randomly choose one sock from a drawer of 6 white and 6 black socks.

You choose a white sock or you choose a black sock.

**c.** A runner competes in a race.

The runner comes in first, the runner comes in second, the runner comes in third, or the runner does not place.

# Additional Practice: Digital Assessments

**7.** There are two marbles of the same size in a bag, one red and one green. Suppose you pick a marble, record the color, and replace the marble in the bag. Which of the following statements are true? *Select all that apply.*

☐ If you pick a marble 100 times, you would expect to have picked red 75 times.

☐ If you pick a marble 20 times, you would expect to have picked a red marble 10 times and a green marble 10 times.

☐ If you pick a marble 8 times and get results of RGRGRGRG, it is highly likely that the next marble you pick will be red.

☐ If the red marble is larger than the green marble, then each marble is equally likely to be picked.

**8.** Carmelo emptied 50 coins from his wallet onto a table. Assuming the coins are fair coins, circle the numbers that make each statement true.

Carmelo can expect $\begin{bmatrix} 0 \\ 10 \\ 25 \\ 40 \\ 50 \end{bmatrix}$ coins to show heads and $\begin{bmatrix} 0 \\ 10 \\ 25 \\ 40 \\ 50 \end{bmatrix}$ coins to show tails.

If he flips one of the coins 10 times, it is likely that $\begin{bmatrix} \frac{1}{10} \\ \frac{1}{5} \\ \frac{1}{2} \end{bmatrix}$ of the time, the coin will land on tails.

**9.** Decide whether each situation describes equally likely results or not equally likely results by placing their letter in the correct box.

| A) Choosing ice cream from the flavor choices chocolate, mint chip, or cookies and cream | B) Rolling a fair number cube and it lands on an even or odd number | C) Drawing winning ticket or a losing ticket from a bin of 100 winning and 100 losing tickets | D) Picking Celia, Tré, or Angelo to be your partner in PE class |
|---|---|---|---|

| **Equally Likely** | **Not Equally Likely** |
|---|---|
| | |

# Additional Practice

**1.** An ordinary 6-sided number cube has the numbers from 1 through 6 on its faces.

  **a.** If you roll a 6-sided number cube, what are the possible outcomes?

  **b.** Suppose you roll a 6-sided number cube 18 times. How many times would you expect to roll a 5? What are you assuming about the possible outcomes?

  **c.** Takashi and Glen are playing a game. For each turn, a number cube is rolled. If the roll is an even number, Takashi gets a point. If the roll is odd, Glen gets a point. Is this a fair game? Explain.

**2.** Patrick counted the cars that drove by his house over a 5-minute period. He counted a total of 27 cars.

  **a.** If Patrick had counted cars for an hour, about how many would you expect him to have counted?

  **b.** Suppose that at the same time of the day exactly one week later, Patrick counts cars over a 20-minute period. About how many cars would you expect him to count?

  **c.** If Patrick started counting cars after school at about 3 P.M., would you expect him to count more, fewer, or about the same number of cars than if he started counting at 5 P.M.? Explain your reasoning.

# Additional Practice (continued)

3. A bag contains 20 pieces of candy. There are 8 grape pieces, 7 cherry pieces, and 5 lemon pieces.

   a. One piece is drawn from the bag. Find the theoretical probability of drawing each flavor.

      i. P(grape)       ii. P(cherry)       iii. P(lemon)

   b. Write each of the probabilities from part (a) as a percent.

      i. P(grape)       ii. P(cherry)       iii. P(lemon)

   c. Suppose 2 grape pieces, 1 cherry piece, and 1 lemon piece are removed from the bag. What is the theoretical probability of drawing each flavor now?

      i. P(grape)       ii. P(cherry)       iii. P(lemon)

   d. In part (c), what is the theoretical probability of *not* drawing lemon?

4. A can contains 8 chips. Three chips are gray, 4 are checkered, and 1 is white.

   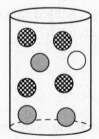

   a. What is the probability of drawing a white chip?

   b. What is the probability of drawing a checkered chip?

   c. What is the probability of drawing a gray chip?

   d. What is the probability of *not* drawing a white chip?

   e. What is the probability of *not* drawing a gray chip?

# Additional Practice (continued)

**5.** A bucket contains 24 blocks. Some are blue, some are green, some are red, and some are yellow. The theoretical probabilities of drawing a blue, green, or red block are:

$$P(\text{blue}) = \tfrac{1}{12}, P(\text{green}) = \tfrac{1}{8}, P(\text{red}) = \tfrac{1}{3}.$$

**a.** How many blue blocks are in the bucket?

**b.** How many green blocks are in the bucket?

**c.** How many red blocks are in the bucket?

**d.** How many yellow blocks are in the bucket?

**e.** What is the probability of drawing a yellow block?

**f.** What is the probability of *not* drawing a yellow block?

**6.** If you roll two number cubes and add the results, which is more likely, getting an even sum or getting an odd sum? Explain.

**7.** If you roll one number cube and add the numbers on the top and bottom faces, which is more likely, getting an even sum or getting an odd sum? Explain.

**8.** If you roll one number cube, is it more likely that the number rolled is a prime number or a non-prime number? Explain.

**9.** A radio station is giving away grab bags that each contain a shirt and some station advertisements. The shirts come in four sizes: small, medium, large, and extra-large; and in three colors: red, blue, or gray. They also can be either short-sleeved or long-sleeved. Each shirt combination is equally likely to be in a grab bag.

   **a.** Make a tree diagram to determine how many different shirt options are possible.

   **b.** What is the probability that a chosen bag will contain a large blue shirt with short sleeves? Explain your reasoning.

   **c.** What is the probability that a chosen bag will contain a small red shirt? Explain.

**10.** Students have earned 36 reward tickets which are placed in a bag to draw from. Some are game choice, some are seat swap, some are PJ day, and some are student's choice. The theoretical probabilities of picking a game choice, seat swap, and PJ day are:

$$P(\text{game choice}) = \frac{1}{3} \qquad P(\text{seat swap}) = \frac{1}{4} \qquad P(\text{PJ day}) = \frac{1}{9}$$

Which of the following statements are true? *Select all that apply.*

☐ There are 9 seat swap reward tickets.

☐ There are 10 student's choice reward tickets.

☐ The probability of not picking a student's choice reward ticket is $\frac{25}{36}$.

☐ There are 3 seat swap reward tickets.

**11.** A number cube with the numbers 1, 2, 3, 4, 5, and 6 is rolled once. Circle the probability of rolling each of the following:

**a.** rolling a 3: $\begin{bmatrix} \frac{1}{2} \\ \frac{1}{3} \\ \frac{1}{6} \end{bmatrix}$

**b.** rolling a number greater than 2: $\begin{bmatrix} \frac{1}{2} \\ \frac{1}{3} \\ \frac{2}{3} \end{bmatrix}$

**c.** rolling a number greater than 6: $\begin{bmatrix} 0 \\ \frac{1}{6} \\ 1 \end{bmatrix}$

**d.** rolling a number less than 7: $\begin{bmatrix} 0 \\ \frac{1}{6} \\ 1 \end{bmatrix}$

**e.** rolling an odd number: $\begin{bmatrix} \frac{1}{2} \\ \frac{1}{3} \\ \frac{1}{6} \end{bmatrix}$

# Skill: Probability

**A number cube is rolled once. Find each probability and write it as a fraction, decimal, and percent.**

**1.** $P(3)$

**2.** $P(\text{even})$

**3.** $P(1, 3, \text{or } 5)$

**4.** $P(0)$

**5.** $P(1 \text{ or } 6)$

**6.** $P(1 \text{ through } 6)$

**A stack of 9 cards is placed face down. Each card has one letter of the word EXCELLENT. Find each probability and write it as a fraction, decimal, and percent.**

**7.** $P(\text{E})$

**8.** $P(\text{N})$

**9.** $P(\text{T or X})$

**10.** $P(\text{consonant})$

**There are 8 blue marbles, 9 orange marbles, and 6 yellow marbles in a bag. You draw one marble. Find each probability and write it as a fraction and percent.**

**11.** $P(\text{blue marble})$

**12.** $P(\text{yellow marble})$

**13.** What marble could you add or remove so that the probability of drawing a blue marble is $\frac{1}{3}$?

# Skill: Probability (continued)

A box contains 12 slips of paper as shown.
Each slip of paper is equally likely to be drawn.
Find each probability.

| red | blue | yellow | blue |
|-----|------|--------|------|
| yellow | red | blue | red |
| red | red | red | yellow |

**14.** $P$(red)

**15.** $P$(blue)

**16.** $P$(yellow)

**17.** $P$(red) + $P$(blue)

**18.** $P$(red) + $P$(yellow)

**19.** $P$(blue) + $P$(yellow)

**20.** $P$(red or blue)

**21.** $P$(red or yellow)

**22.** $P$(blue or yellow)

**23.** $P$(not red)

**24.** $P$(not blue)

**25.** $P$(not yellow)

# Additional Practice

**What Do You Expect?**

**Use your angle ruler and the spinner at the right to answer the questions in Exercises 1 and 2.**

1. Determine the probability of landing in each part (region) of the spinner.

   **a.** gray

   **b.** checked

   **c.** diagonal lines

   **d.** wavy lines

   **e.** unmarked

2. You spin the spinner 40 times. How many times would you expect it to land in each of these regions?

   **a.** diagonal lines

   **b.** gray

   **c.** unmarked

3. Ralph would like to make a spinner with three regions colored black, white, and yellow. He wants to make it so that you could expect to spin black $\frac{1}{2}$ of the time, yellow $\frac{1}{3}$ of the time, and white $\frac{1}{4}$ of the time. Is it possible to make such a spinner? Explain.

4. Glenda has designed a spinner with blue, red, and green sections. The chances of spinning blue on Glenda's spinner are 50%, the chances of spinning red are 20%, and the chances of spinning green are 30%. Suppose you spin Glenda's spinner 50 times.

   **a.** How many times would you expect to spin blue?

   **b.** How many times would you expect to spin red?

   **c.** How many times would you expect to spin green?

# Additional Practice (continued)

**5.** Use the spinner at the right to answer the following questions.

   **a.** What fraction of the spinner is shaded gray?

   **b.** What fraction is unshaded?

   **c.** What fraction is marked with diagonal lines?

   **d.** Suppose you spin the spinner 72 times.

     **i.** How many times would you expect to spin gray?

     **ii.** How many times would you expect to spin the unshaded region?

     **iii.** How many times would you expect to spin diagonals?

**6.** A game called *Part or Whole?* uses the two spinners shown at the right.

One player spins Spinner A and the other spins Spinner B. The number spun on Spinner A is then divided by the number spun on Spinner B. If the result is a fraction, the player spinning Spinner A gets a point. If the quotient is a whole number, the player spinning Spinner B gets a point.

Spinner A       Spinner B

   **a.** List all the possible number pairs that can be spun with two spinners and find the quotient of each pair.

   **b.** Is *Part or Whole?* a fair game? Explain your reasoning.

   **c.** What is the probability of spinning a quotient of 1?

   **d.** What is the probability of spinning a quotient of 3?

   **e.** What is the probability of *not* spinning a quotient of $\frac{2}{3}$?

# Additional Practice (continued)

**7.** In which spinners below are the outcomes 1, 2, 3, and 4 equally likely? Explain.

 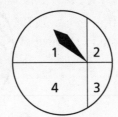 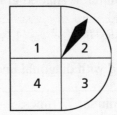

**8.** Assuming that it is equally likely for a person to be born with brown eyes or with eyes that are not brown, answer the following questions.

**a.** What are all the possible outcomes (that is, having brown eyes or not) for two children? List the outcomes in the form (eye color of first child, eye color of second child).

**b.** What is the probability that both children have brown eyes?

**c.** What is the probability that one child has brown eyes and the other does not?

**d.** What is the probability that the oldest child has brown eyes?

**9.** Assuming that it is equally likely for a child to be born with brown eyes or with eyes that are not brown, answer the following questions.

**a.** Suppose a family has three children. List all the possible outcomes for the eye colors of the children.

**b.** If a family has three children, what is the probability that all three children have brown eyes? That all three children do not have brown eyes?

**c.** What is the probability of having two children with brown eyes and one child with eyes that are not brown?

**d.** What is the probability of having two children with eyes that are not brown and one child with brown eyes?

**e.** Josh and his younger brother both have brown eyes.. What is the probability that a third child will have brown eyes? Explain.

# Additional Practice (continued)

10. Assuming that it is equally likely for a child to be born with brown eyes or with eyes that are not brown, answer the following questions.

   a. A family has one child. Describe a simulation that could be used to find the experimental probability of the child having brown eyes. Explain your choice.

   b. Susan would like to have four children. Describe a simulation she could use to find the experimental probability that, given she does have four children, two have brown eyes and two do not. Explain your choice.

11. Here are two spinners. Suppose you spin both spinners.

   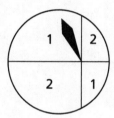 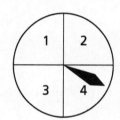

   a. Make a chart or other diagram to show all of the outcomes.

   b. Are the outcomes equally likely? If not, which ones are most likely and which ones are least likely? Explain your thinking.

   c. Suppose you spin the spinners and add the numbers. Make a list of the possible sums.

   d. Are the sums equally likely? Explain.

# Additional Practice *(continued)*

**12.** The *Four-by-Four* game has a game piece with four congruent triangular faces numbered 1, 2, 3, and 4. The result of a roll is the number on the face touching the table. To play the game, players take turns rolling two game pieces and adding the results. If the sum is odd, the first player gets a point. If the sum is even, the second player gets a point.

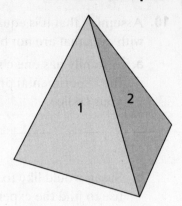

**a.** List all the possible number pairs that can be rolled and the sum for each pair.

**b.** Is *Four-by-Four* a fair game? Explain your reasoning.

**c.** Which sum is most likely, and what is its probability?

**d.** What is the probability of rolling a sum of 6?

**e.** What is the probability of rolling a sum of 3?

**f.** What is the probability of *not* rolling a sum of 8? Explain.

## Additional Practice (continued)

13. A game is played by rolling a 4-sided game piece with faces numbered 1, 2, 3, 4 and a 6-sided number cube with faces numbered 1, 2, 3, 4, 5, 6 and finding the sum of the numbers rolled.

   A player wins by rolling a sum of 2, 3, 4, 9, or 10; otherwise, the player loses.

   a. List all the possible number pairs that can be rolled and find the sum of each pair.

   b. Is this game fair or unfair? Explain your reasoning.

   c. What is the probability of rolling a sum of 7?

   d. What is the probability of rolling a sum of 4?

   e. What is the probability of rolling a sum of 9?

   f. If you played this game 48 times, how many times would you expect to win? How many times would you expect to lose?

   g. Suppose the game costs 25 rubas to play, and if you win you get 50 rubas. Suppose you play the game 48 times. Use your answers from part (f) to answer the following questions:

   i. How many rubas would it cost to play 48 times?

   ii. How many rubas would you expect to win?

   iii. How many rubas would you expect to win or lose overall after playing the game 48 times?

# Additional Practice: Digital Assessments

**14.** Assume it is equally likely for a student to have A lunch period or B lunch period. In a group of three friends, which of the following statements are true?

*Select all that apply.*

☐ The probability that all three friends have A lunch period is $\frac{1}{2}$.

☐ The probability that one student has A lunch period and the other two have B lunch period is $\frac{3}{8}$.

☐ There is an equally likely chance that all three students have A lunch period or that all three students have B lunch period.

☐ The probability that the youngest student has B lunch period is $\frac{1}{4}$.

**15.** A jar contains 12 pieces of paper with one letter on each piece of paper. The letters are A, B, C, D, E, F, G, H, I, J, K, and L. You randomly pick two pieces of paper from the jar. Find the probability of each result by using the numbers on the tiles.

| $\frac{1}{4}$ | $\frac{1}{12}$ | $\frac{1}{16}$ | $\frac{1}{144}$ |
|---|---|---|---|
| $\frac{3}{16}$ | $\frac{9}{12}$ | $\frac{9}{16}$ | $1$ |

**a.** P(A, then A) = ☐

**b.** P(vowel, then consonant) = ☐

**c.** P(consonant, then consonant) = ☐

**d.** P(consonant, then I) = ☐

**16.** A spinner has five regions. There is a $\frac{1}{9}$ chance of landing on A, a $\frac{5}{36}$ chance of landing on B, a $\frac{1}{6}$ chance of landing on C, a $\frac{1}{4}$ chance of landing on D, and a $\frac{1}{3}$ chance of landing on E. Suppose you spin the spinner 50 times and record each result. Circle the number that makes each statement true.

**a.** It is likely that you landed on C about $\begin{bmatrix} 6 \\ 8 \\ 30 \end{bmatrix}$ times.

**b.** It is likely that you landed on B about $\begin{bmatrix} 7 \\ 10 \\ 25 \end{bmatrix}$ times.

**c.** It is likely that you landed on D or E about $\begin{bmatrix} 4 \\ 17 \\ 29 \end{bmatrix}$ times.

# Skill: Experimental and Theoretical Probability

Each shape in a set of blocks comes in two sizes (small and large), three colors (yellow, red, and blue), and two thicknesses (thick and thin). There is exactly one block with each combination of the three attributes.

1. Draw a tree diagram to find the total number of outcomes for randomly drawing one of these blocks.

2. How many outcomes are possible?

3. How many outcomes will be red?

4. How many outcomes will be blue and thin?

5. How many outcomes will be large?

6. Suppose a medium size is also available. How many outcomes are possible now?

A box contains ten balls, numbered 1 through 10. Marisha draws a ball. She records its number and then returns it to the bag. Then Penney draws a ball. Find each probability.

7. $P(9, \text{then } 3)$

8. $P(\text{even, then odd})$

9. $P(\text{odd, then } 2)$

10. $P(\text{the sum of the numbers is } 25)$

11. $P(\text{a factor of } 8, \text{then a multiple of } 2)$

# Additional Practice

**1.** Shawon has a spinner that is divided into four regions. He spins the spinner several times and records his results in a table.

| Region | Number of Times Spinner Lands in Region |
|--------|------------------------------------------|
| 1      | 9                                        |
| 2      | 4                                        |
| 3      | 12                                       |
| 4      | 11                                       |

**a.** Based on Shawon's results, what is the probability of the spinner landing on region 1?

**b.** What is the probability of the spinner landing on region 2?

**c.** What is the probability of the spinner landing on region 3?

**d.** What is the probability of the spinner landing on region 4?

**e.** Are the probabilities you found in parts (a)–(d) theoretical probabilities or experimental probabilities?

**f.** Make a drawing of what Shawon's spinner might look like.

# Additional Practice (continued)

2. Irene randomly tosses a cube onto the grid below. Express the probability of each outcome as a percent.

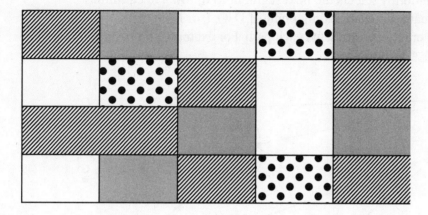

a. What is the probability of the cube landing on a striped rectangle?

b. What is the probability of the cube landing on a white rectangle?

c. What is the probability of the cube landing on a gray rectangle?

d. What is the probability of the cube landing on a dotted rectangle?

e. What is the probability of the cube *not* landing on a white rectangle?

f. What is the probability of the cube *not* landing on a striped rectangle?

g. Irene proposed the following game: If the cube lands on a striped square or a dotted square, Irene wins; if the cube lands on a white square or a gray square, Irene's sister wins. Is this a fair game? Explain your reasoning.

# Additional Practice (continued)

**3.** Zark is walking from point A to the end of the paths. He can only travel to the right. Starting at point A, he randomly picks a path to follow. When he reaches a lettered point, he randomly selects the next segment to follow. He continues this process until he reaches the an ending point of D, G, I, or N. In parts (a)–(e) below, a series of letters represents each path. For example, the path *AEJI* is the path from *A* to *E* to *J* to *I*.

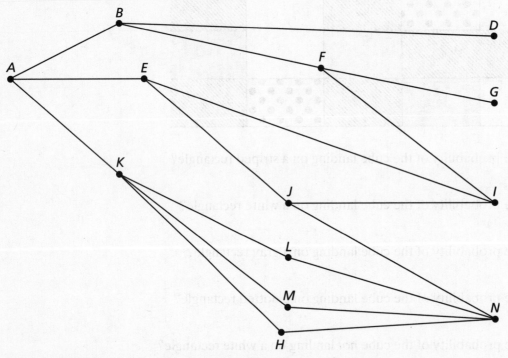

**a.** What is the probability that Zark followed path *AEJN*?

**b.** What is the probability that he followed path *ABD*?

**c.** What is the probability that he followed path *ABFI*?

**d.** Are paths *AKLN* and *AKMN* equally likely to be selected? Explain your reasoning.

**e.** If Zark repeats this process 50 times, how many times would you expect him to follow path *AEJI*? Explain.

**4. a.** If a letter is randomly selected from the letters A, B, C, D, and E, what is the probability that the letter will be B? Explain.

**b.** If a letter is selected by spinning the spinner at the right, what is the probability that the letter will be B? Explain.

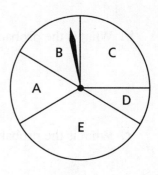

**c.** Are your answers to parts (a) and (b) the same? Explain.

**d.** If the spinner is spun once, what is the probability that it will *not* land in region C? Explain.

**e.** If the spinner is spun once, what is the probability that it will land in region D? Explain.

**f.** If the spinner is spun 100 times, how many times would you expect it to land in region E? Explain.

# Additional Practice *(continued)*

5. The faces of one 6-sided number cube are labeled 1, 1, 1, 2, 2, 3, and the faces of a second cube are labeled 0, 1, 2, 2, 2, 3. The two cubes are rolled, and the results are added.

   **a.** What is the probability of rolling a sum of 1?

   **b.** What is the probability of rolling a sum of 6?

   **c.** What is the probability of rolling a sum of 4?

   **d.** What is the probability of rolling a sum that is *not* 1 or 6? Explain.

6. **a.** Jennifer is on her school's softball team. So far this season, Jennifer has 38 hits in 75 times at bat. Based on her current batting average, what are Jennifer's chances of getting a hit next time she is at bat? Explain your reasoning.

   **b.** If Jennifer bats 5 times during a game, how many hits would you expect her to get? Explain.

   **c.** Next season, Jennifer wants to average 6 hits for every 10 times at bat. If she bats 80 times during the season, how many hits will she need to get to achieve her goal?

## Additional Practice (continued)

7. Aaron bowls on his school's bowling team. Based on statistics from past games, the probability that Aaron will knock down all 10 pins on his first ball (a strike) is $\frac{2}{5}$. If he does not get a strike, the probability that he will knock down the remaining pins with his second ball (a spare) is $\frac{3}{4}$.

   **a.** In bowling, a turkey is 3 strikes in a row. If Aaron bowls 3 turns, what is the probability that he will get a turkey?

   **b.** Aaron had 8 chances to make spares during one of his league games. How many of the spares would you expect him to have made? Explain.

   **c.** In bowling, an open occurs when the bowler does not get a strike on the first ball and then does not get a spare on the second ball. When Aaron rolls 2 balls, what are his chances of getting an open?

   **d.** Suppose Aaron bowls 30 practice frames. When he does not get a strike, he tries to get a spare.

   **i.** How many strikes would you expect Aaron to get?

   **ii.** How many spares would you expect Aaron to get?

   **iii.** How many opens would you expect Aaron to get?

# Additional Practice (continued)

8. In a game, two players take turns rolling two number cubes, each numbered 1 to 6. The numbers are added, and the sum is multiplied by 6. If the final result is an odd number, Player I gets 1 point. If the final result is an even number, Player II gets 1 point.

   **a.** List all the possible outcomes of a turn (that is, list the final results when the sum of two number cubes is multiplied by 6).

   **b.** What is the probability that the final number will be odd? What is the probability that the final number will be even? Explain.

   **c.** Is this a fair game?

9. The *Alphabet Game* costs $0.25 to play. Before the game, 26 slips of paper, each with a different letter of the alphabet on it, are put into a bag. A player draws one slip from the bag. If the player draws a vowel (A, E, I, O, or U), he or she wins $1.

   **a.** What is the probability of winning the game?

   **b.** What is the probability of losing the game?

   **c.** If a player plays the *Alphabet Game* 26 times, how much money would you expect the player to win or lose? Explain.

**182**

## Additional Practice (continued)

10. Suppose you play a game in which you toss 1 coin. You win $10 if it lands HEADS and you win nothing if it lands TAILS.

    a. If it costs $5 to play the game, would you expect to win or lose money in the long run? Explain.

    b. If it costs $10 to play the game, would you expect people to want to play the game? Explain.

    c. If it costs $6 to play the game, would you expect people to want to play the game? Explain.

    d. If it costs $4 to play the game, would you expect people to want to play the game? Explain.

# Additional Practice: Digital Assessments

**11.** Anton wrote a computer program that assigns one of four numbers to each table cell according to predetermined probabilities. He ran the program once and obtained the result shown below. Which of the following statements are true? *Select all that apply.*

| A | B | C | D |
|---|---|---|---|
| C | B | A | B |
| B | C | D | B |
| B | D | B | C |

☐ According to the results, each letter was equally likely to get chosen.

☐ If a similar design with 64 rectangles was lettered using the same program, Anton can expect to have 12 "D" rectangles.

☐ If Anton uses the same program to letter a new design and wants to have 20 "C" rectangles, then the design should be made up of 80 rectangles.

☐ If a logo is to be randomly placed on one of the rectangles in the above design, the probability that it is on a "B" rectangle is 43.75%.

**12.** Elizabeth rolls a number cube and then spins a spinner. The number cube is numbered 2, 3, 4, 5, 6, and 7 and the spinner has 4 equal sections numbered 1, 2, 3, and 4. Find each probability by using the numbers on the tiles.

$\frac{1}{6}$  $\frac{1}{3}$  $\frac{1}{24}$  $\frac{1}{2}$

$\frac{5}{6}$  75%  25%  20%

**a.** P(rolling a 2, spinning a 3) = ☐

**b.** P(sum is greater than 8) = ☐

**c.** P(sum is even) = ☐

**d.** P(sum is not 6) = ☐

**13.** Campbell plays on his school's basketball team. He has made 16 out of 25 free throws this season. Complete each statement by circling the correct number.

**a.** Based on his current percentage, the probability of Campbell making his next

free throw is $\begin{bmatrix} 16\% \\ 36\% \\ 64\% \end{bmatrix}$.

**b.** If Campbell gets to the free throw line three times in his next game, you would

expect him to make $\begin{bmatrix} 0 \\ 1 \\ 2 \\ 3 \end{bmatrix}$ free throws.

# Skill: Area Models and Probability

**A spinner is divided into 5 equal sections. You spin the spinner once.**

**1.** Find the probability that the spinner lands on a white section.

**2.** Find the probability that the spinner lands on a dark section.

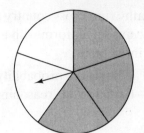

**A dart is thrown at the game board shown. The larger sections of the dart board are congruent to each other and include a right angle. The smaller sections are congruent to each other. Find each probability.**

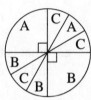

**3.** *P(A)*

**4.** *P(B)*

**5.** *P(C)*

**6.** *P*(not *A*)

**7.** *P*(not *B*)

**8.** *P*(not *C*)

# Additional Practice

1. Kathy runs cross country and plays basketball and softball. For each sport, she received a uniform with a randomly assigned number between 0 and 99 printed on it.

   a. What is the probability that all of Kathy's uniforms have odd numbers? Explain your reasoning.

   b. What is the probability that all of Kathy's uniforms have even numbers?

   c. What is the probability that one of Kathy's uniforms has an even number and the other two have odd numbers?

2. To play the *Nickel Game*, a player tosses two nickels at the same time. If both nickels land tails up, the player wins $1. If both nickels land heads up, the player wins $2. Otherwise, the player wins nothing.

   a. It costs $1 to play the *Nickel Game*. How much should a player expect to win or lose if he or she plays the game 12 times? Explain.

   b. At next year's carnival, the game committee wants to charge prices that will allow players to break even. How much should they charge to play the *Nickel Game*? Explain.

3. In the *Ring Toss* game, a player tosses a ring at a group of bottles. If the ring goes over a bottle, the player wins a prize. The attendant at the *Ring Toss* game tells Ben that his chances of winning are 50% because when Ben tosses a ring, it will either go over a bottle or it will not. Do you believe the attendant? Explain.

## Additional Practice (continued)

4. Two teams, Eagles and Falcons, are going to play a championship series of 3 games. The teams are evenly matched, so they have the same chance of winning each game.

   **a.** What is the probability that the Eagles win the first game? The Falcons?

   **b.** If the Eagles win the first game, what is the probability that the Eagles win the second game? The Falcons?

   **c.** If the Eagles win the first game, what is the probability that the series ends in two games?

   **d.** If the Eagles win the first game and the Falcons win the second game, what is the probability that the Eagles win the series?

   **e.** If the Eagles win the first game and the Falcons win the second game, what is the probability that the Falcons win the series?

5. Suppose the Eagles are twice as likely as the Falcons to win each game.

   **a.** What is the probability that the Eagles win the first game? The Falcons?

   **b.** If the Eagles win the first game, what is the probability that the Eagles win the second game? The Falcons?

   **c.** If the Eagles win the first game, what is the probability that the series ends in two games?

   **d.** If the Eagles win the first game and the Falcons win the second game, what is the probability that the Eagles win the series?

   **e.** If the Eagles win the first game and the Falcons win the second game, what is the probability that the Falcons win the series?

# Additional Practice (continued)

**6. a.** Suppose the Crawfords have three children. Assume that the probability of a child being born with brown eyes (B) or with eyes that are not brown (N) is $\frac{1}{2}$ for each birth. List the possible outcomes.

**b.** What is the probability that exactly two of the Crawfords' children have brown eyes and are born in a row?

**c.** What is the probability that the Crawfords have at least two children with brown eyes born in a row?

**d.** Explain why the answers to parts (b) and (c) are not the same.

**7. a.** Suppose the Crawfords have four children. Assume that the probability of a a child being born with brown eyes (B) or with eyes that are not brown (N) is $\frac{1}{2}$ for each birth. List the possible outcomes.

**b.** What is the probability that exactly two of the Crawfords' children have brown eyes and are born in a row?

**c.** What is the probability that the Crawfords have at least two children with brown eyes born in a row?

**d.** Explain why the answers to parts (b) and (c) are not the same.

# Additional Practice: Digital Assessments

**8.** The Bears and Hawks are playing a three-game series against each other. Which of the following statements are true? *Select all that apply.*

☐ If the teams are evenly matched, meaning they both have the same chance at winning, the probability of the Bears winning the second game is $\frac{1}{4}$.

☐ If the teams are evenly matched and the Hawks win the first game, the probability of the Bears winning the second game is $\frac{1}{2}$.

☐ If the Bears are three times more likely to win, the probability of the Hawks winning the first game is $\frac{1}{4}$.

☐ If the Bears are three times more likely to win, the probability of the Bears winning the first game is $\frac{3}{4}$.

**9.** Jerome was assigned a random six-number identification code with the numbers ranging from 1 to 10. Numbers can be repeated. Complete each statement using the fractions on the tiles. Tiles may be used more than once.

| $\frac{1}{4}$ | $\frac{1}{16}$ | $\frac{1}{32}$ | $\frac{1}{64}$ |
|---|---|---|---|
| $\frac{3}{4}$ | $\frac{15}{16}$ | $\frac{31}{32}$ | $\frac{63}{64}$ |

**a.** The probability that at least one number is even is ⬜.

**b.** The probability that all six numbers are even is ⬜.

**c.** Jerome sees that the first number is a 5. The probability that the remaining numbers are all odd is ⬜.

**10.** A game at a carnival consists of spinning the spinner at the right two times. If a player lands on an even number both times, the player wins $4. If a player lands on an even number first and then an odd number, the player wins $1. Otherwise, the player wins nothing. It costs $1 to play the game.

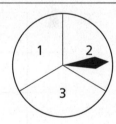

Complete each statement by circling the correct answers.

**a.** A player plays the game 18 times. The player can expect to $\begin{bmatrix} \text{win} \\ \text{lose} \end{bmatrix}$ about $\begin{bmatrix} \$3 \\ \$6 \\ \$13 \end{bmatrix}$.

**b.** If the ticket price was between $\begin{bmatrix} \$0.25 - \$0.50 \\ \$0.50 - \$0.75 \\ \$0.75 - \$1.00 \end{bmatrix}$, it would take about 18 games to break even.

# Additional Practice

1. The four nets below will fold into rectangular boxes. Net *iii* folds into an open box. The other nets fold into closed boxes. Answer the following questions for each net.

   a. What are the dimensions of the box that can be made from the net?

   b. What is the surface area of the box?

   c. What total number of unit cubes would be needed to fill the box?

   **i.**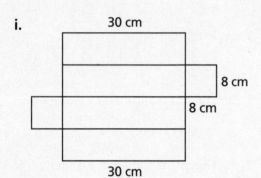

   **ii.**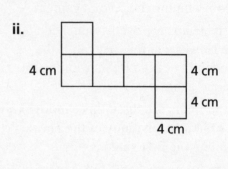

   **iii.**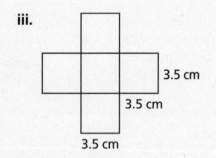

   **iv.**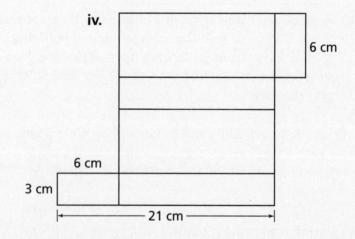

## Additional Practice (continued)

**2. a.** Gina has a sheet of cardboard that measures 9 feet by 6 feet. She uses scissors and tape to make the entire sheet of cardboard into a closed box that is a perfect cube. What is the surface area of the box?

**b.** What is the length of each edge of the box? Explain your reasoning.

**c.** How many unit cubes would it take to fill the box?

**3. a.** Bill has a sheet of cardboard with an area of 10 square feet. He makes the entire sheet of cardboard into a closed rectangular box. The four sides of the box have the same area, and the two ends have the same area. The area of each of the four equal sides is twice the area of each end. What is the area of each face of Bill's box?

**b.** What are the dimensions of Bill's box?

**c.** How many unit cubes would it take to fill the box?

# Additional Practice *(continued)*

**4.** For each given volume, find the dimensions of the box that uses the least amount of packaging material. Round to the nearest 0.1 centimeter.

   **a.** 4,000 cubic centimeters

   **b.** 300 cubic centimeters

**5.** Kirk has a compost box with dimensions 1 foot by 2 feet by 2 feet. He wants to increase the size of his compost box.

   **a.** What are the surface area and volume of the original box?

   **b.** What change in dimensions would give the box twice the volume of the original?

   **c.** If you double each dimension, what are the surface area and volume of the new box?

   **d.** Kirk builds a new compost box similar to the original box. The volume of the new box is 256 cubic feet. What scale factor did he use to build the new box?

# Additional Practice: Digital Assessments

**6.** Carey has a box with dimensions 2 feet by 3 feet by 2 feet. Which of the following statements are true? *Select all that apply.*

☐ The surface area of the box is 12 ft².

☐ The volume of the box is 12 ft³.

☐ Increasing the longest dimension by 3 feet will double the volume of the box.

☐ Doubling every dimension of the box will double the surface area.

☐ Doubling every dimension of the box will double the volume.

**7.** Use the values on the tiles to write an equation for the area of the figure.

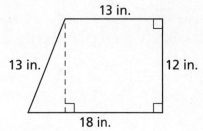

**8.** Circle the numbers and formulas that complete the description of how you can find the area of the triangle below.

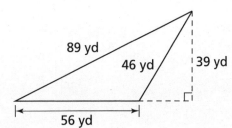

The area of a triangle is given by the formula $\begin{bmatrix} A = lw \\ A = \frac{1}{2}\,bh \\ A = \pi r^2 \end{bmatrix}$. The height of the triangle

is $\begin{bmatrix} 39 \\ 46 \\ 56 \\ 89 \end{bmatrix}$ yards.

The base of the triangle is $\begin{bmatrix} 46 \\ 56 \\ 89 \end{bmatrix}$ yards. Therefore, the area of the triangle is

$\begin{bmatrix} 897 \\ 1,092 \\ 2,184 \end{bmatrix}$ square yards.

Name _____ Date _____ Class _____

# Skill: Area Review

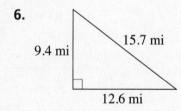

**Find the area of each figure.**

**1.**
4 m

4 m

**2.**
5 cm

23 cm

**3.**
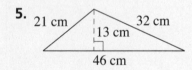
5 in.    4 in.

8 in.

**4.**
8 mm
10 mm
10 mm

**5.**
21 cm    32 cm
13 cm
46 cm

**6.**
9.4 mi    15.7 mi

12.6 mi

**7.**
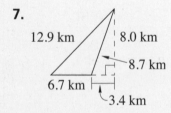
12.9 km    8.0 km

8.7 km

6.7 km

3.4 km

**8.**
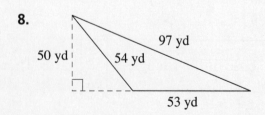
97 yd
50 yd    54 yd

53 yd

# Skill: Area Review (continued)

**Find the area of each figure.**

**9.**
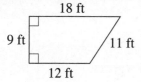

18 ft

9 ft    11 ft

12 ft

**10.**
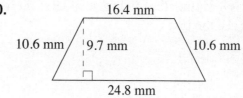

16.4 mm

10.6 mm    9.7 mm    10.6 mm

24.8 mm

**11.**
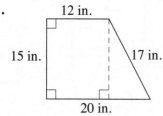

12 in.

15 in.    17 in.

20 in.

**12.**
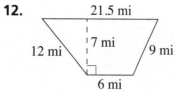

21.5 mi

12 mi    7 mi    9 mi

6 mi

**13.**
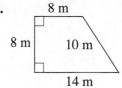

8 m

8 m    10 m

14 m

**14.**
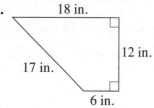

18 in.

17 in.    12 in.

6 in.

# Additional Practice

1. The bottom of a closed rectangular box has an area of 30 square centimeters. If the box is 8 centimeters high, give at least three possibilities for the dimensions of the box.

2. **a.** The rectangular prism at the right is made from centimeter cubes. What are the dimensions of the prism?

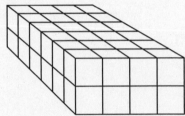

 **b.** What is the surface area of the prism?

 **c.** What is the volume of the prism? That is, how many cubes are in the prism?

 **d.** Give the dimensions of a different rectangular prism that can be made from the same number of cubes. What is the surface area of the prism?

## Additional Practice (continued)

3. Use the diagram at the right to answer the following questions.

   a. What is the total surface area of the box, including the bottom and the top?

   b. How many 1-inch cubes would it take to fill the box? Explain your reasoning.

3 in.

15 in.

5 in.

4. What is the volume of the prism below? Explain your reasoning.

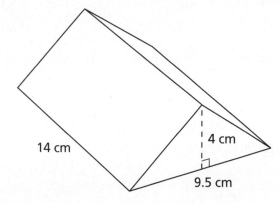

14 cm

4 cm

9.5 cm

5. The volume of a prism is 275 cubic centimeters. The area of the base of the prism is 25 square centimeters. What is the height of the prism? Explain.

# Additional Practice (continued)

**6.** Give the dimensions of three different rectangular prisms that have a volume of 240 cubic centimeters.

**7. a.** Each small cube in the rectangular prism at the right has edges of length 3 centimeters. What are the dimensions of the prism in centimeters?

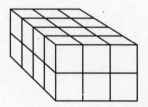

**b.** What is the surface area of the prism in square centimeters?

**c.** How many 1-centimeter cubes would it take to make a prism with the same dimensions as this prism? Explain your reasoning.

# Additional Practice (continued)

**8.** Answer parts (a) and (b) for each closed box below.

   **a.** What is the surface area of each box?

   **i.**

   2 cm

   2 cm   8.5 cm

   **ii.**   5 cm

   11 cm

   5 cm

   **iii.**

   2 cm   9 cm

   7.5 cm

   Box i.

   Box ii.

   Box iii.

   **b.** What is the volume of each box?

   **i.**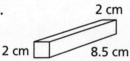

   2 cm

   2 cm   8.5 cm

   **ii.** 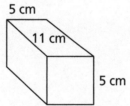  5 cm

   11 cm

   5 cm

   **iii.**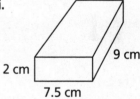

   2 cm   9 cm

   7.5 cm

   Box i.

   Box ii.

   Box iii.

# Additional Practice (continued)

9. Each polygon below is the base of a regular prism whose height is
   8 centimeters. Find the surface area and volume of each prism.
   Round to the nearest 0.1 if needed.

   a.

   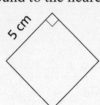

   b.

   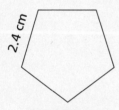

   A = 9.9 sq cm

   c.

   A = 19.3 sq cm

## Additional Practice *(continued)*

**10.** Below are three triangular prisms (not drawn to scale). The height of the first prism is 8 units, and the volumes of all three prisms are the same. What are the heights of the other two prisms?

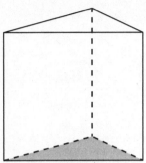

Base of triangle: 6 units
Height of triangle: 2 units

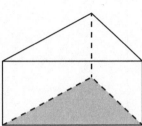

Base of triangle: 6 units
Height of triangle: 4 units

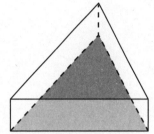

Base of triangle: 6 units
Height of triangle: 8 units

**11.** Below are three triangular prisms (not drawn to scale). The height of the first prism is 8, and the volumes of all three prisms are the same. What are the heights of the other two prisms?

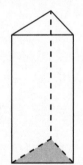

Base of triangle: 6 units
Height of triangle: 2 units

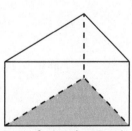

Base of triangle: 12 units
Height of triangle: 4 units

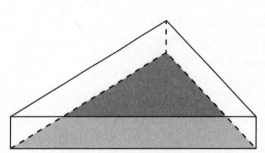

Base of triangle: 24 units
Height of triangle: 8 units

# Additional Practice: Digital Assessments

**12.** Which statements are true about the prism pictured below? *Select all that apply.*

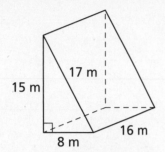

15 m  17 m  8 m  16 m

☐ The surface area of the prism is $(120 + 128 + 240)$ m².

☐ The surface area of the prism is 760 m².

☐ The volume of the prism is $\left(\frac{1}{2}\right)(8)(15)(16)$ m³.

☐ The volume of the prism is 960 cm³.

☐ The volume of the prism is 1,920 m³.

**13.** Use the values on the tiles to write an equation for the volume of the prism.

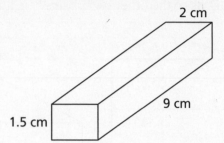

2 cm  9 cm  1.5 cm

1.5    2    9    0.5

13.5    27    +    ×

☐☐☐☐☐ = ☐

**14.** Three prisms are pictured below. All three prisms have the same volume. Use the values from the bank to complete the missing measurements.

2   4   6   8   10   12   14   16

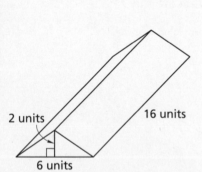

2 units  16 units  6 units

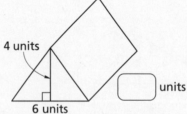

4 units  6 units  ☐ units

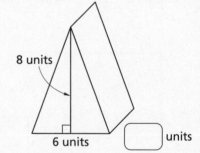

8 units  6 units  ☐ units

Name _____ Date _____ Class _____

# Skill: Surface Area of a Prism

**Draw a net for each prism. Label the dimensions of the net.**

**1.**
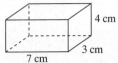
4 cm
3 cm
7 cm

**2.**
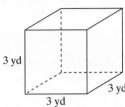
3 yd
3 yd
3 yd

**Find the surface area of each figure to the nearest whole unit.**

**3.**
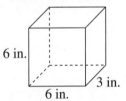
6 in.
6 in.
3 in.

**4.**
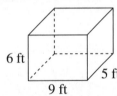
6 ft
9 ft
5 ft

**5.**
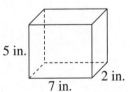
5 in.
7 in.
2 in.

**6.**
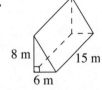
8 m
6 m
15 m

# Skill: Surface Area of a Prism (continued)

**Find the surface area of each prism.**

**7.**

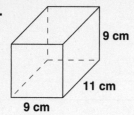

9 cm

11 cm

9 cm

**8.**

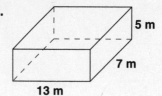

5 m

7 m

13 m

**9.**

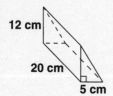

12 cm

20 cm

5 cm

**10.**

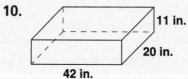

11 in.

20 in.

42 in.

**11.**

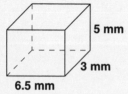

5 mm

3 mm

6.5 mm

**12.**

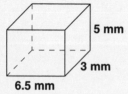

2 in.

8.5 in.

14.5 in.

# Skill: Volume of a Prism

**Find the volume of each prism.**

**1.**

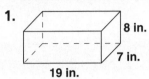

8 in.
7 in.
19 in.

**2.**

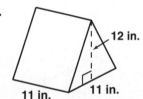

13 ft
12 ft
16 ft
5 ft

**3.**

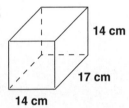

14 cm
17 cm
14 cm

**4.**

12 in.
11 in.
11 in.

# Skill: Volume of a Prism (continued)

**Find the volume of each prism.**

5.

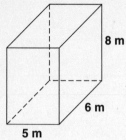

8 m

6 m

5 m

6.

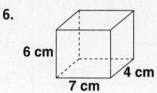

6 cm

7 cm

4 cm

7.

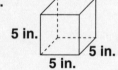

5 in.

5 in.

5 in.

8.

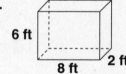

6 ft

8 ft

2 ft

# Additional Practice

**1.** For each of the following, find the circumference and the area of the circle.

**a.**

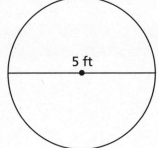

**b.**

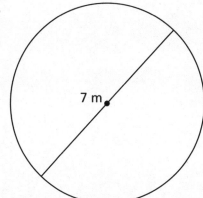

**c.**

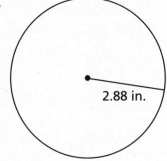

# Additional Practice (continued)

**2.** Use the diagram below to answer the following questions.

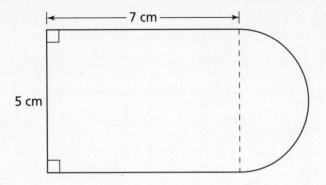

    **a.** What is the perimeter of the figure?

    **b.** What is the area of the figure?

**3.** Use the diagram below to answer the following questions.

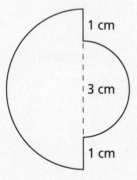

    **a.** What is the perimeter of the figure?

    **b.** What is the area of the figure?

## Additional Practice (continued)

**4.** Below is a diagram of a jogging track. Use the diagram to answer the following questions.

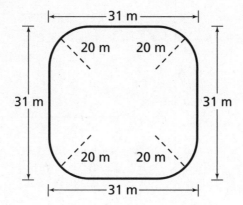

**a.** What is the total distance around the jogging track?

**b.** How much area does the jogging track enclose? Explain your reasoning.

**c.** Suppose Tony wants to jog 4 kilometers. How many times will he have to jog around the track? (Remember that 1,000 meters is 1 kilometer.)

**5.** Which statements are true about the figure pictured below? *Select all that apply.*

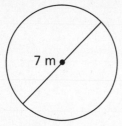

7 m

☐ The circumference of the circle is $C = 2\pi(7)$.

☐ The circumference of the circle is approximately 22 m.

☐ The circumference of the circle is approximately 44 m.

☐ The area of the circle is $A = \pi(7)^2$.

☐ The area of the circle is approximately 38.5 m².

☐ The radius of the circle is 7 m.

**6.** Use the values on the tiles to write an expression for the area of the figure.

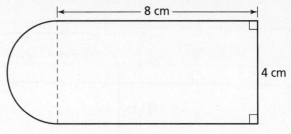

8 cm

4 cm

(5)    (8)    (4)    $\left(\frac{1}{2}\right)$

+    $(4)^2$    $(2)^2$    $(\pi)$

☐ ☐ ☐ ☐ ☐

**7.** Circle the equations or values to explain how you can find the shaded area of the figure.

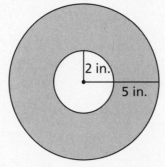

2 in.

5 in.

First, find the area of the larger circle:
$$\begin{bmatrix} (2)(\pi)(5) \approx 31.42 \\ (2)(\pi)(2)^2 \approx 25.12 \\ (\pi)(5)^2 \approx 78.50 \\ (\pi)(2)^2 \approx 12.56 \end{bmatrix}.$$

Then find the area of the smaller circle,
$$\begin{bmatrix} (2)(\pi)(5) \approx 31.42 \\ (2)(\pi)(2)^2 \approx 25.12 \\ (\pi)(5)^2 \approx 78.50 \\ (\pi)(2)^2 \approx 12.56 \end{bmatrix}.$$

Finally, subtract to find that the shaded area is approximately $\begin{bmatrix} 6.29 \\ 18.85 \\ 53.38 \\ 65.94 \end{bmatrix}$ square inches.

# Skill: Area of Circles

**Find the area of each circle. Round to the nearest tenth.**

1.
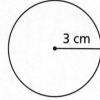
3 cm

2.

2 cm

3.
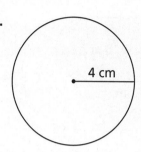
4 cm

**Find the area of each circle. Round to the nearest unit. Use $\frac{22}{7}$ for $\pi$.**

4.
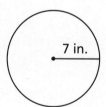
7 in.

5.
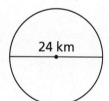
24 km

6.
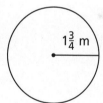
$1\frac{3}{4}$ m

## Skill: Area of Circles (continued)

**Find the area of each shaded region to the nearest tenth.**

**7.**

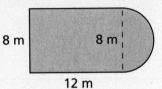

8 m    8 m

12 m

**8.**

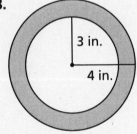

3 in.

4 in.

**9.**

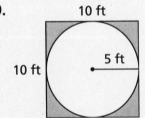

10 ft

5 ft

10 ft

# Additional Practice

**1. a.** The circumference of the base of a cylinder is $16\pi$ centimeters. The height of the cylinder is 10 centimeters. What is the surface area of the cylinder?

**b.** What is the volume of the cylinder?

**2.** Use the closed cylinders below to answer parts (a) and (b). Round your answers to the nearest 0.1.

**i.**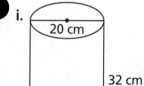
20 cm

32 cm

**ii.**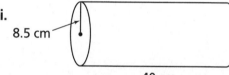
8.5 cm

40 cm

**iii.**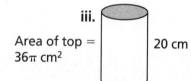
Area of top = $36\pi$ cm²

20 cm

**a.** What is the surface area of each cylinder?

**b.** What is the volume of each cylinder?

## Additional Practice *(continued)*

**3. a.** A cylindrical storage tank has a radius of 1 meter and a height of 3 meters. What is the surface area of the storage tank?

**b.** What is the volume of the storage tank?

**4. a.** A cylinder without a top has a height of 25 centimeters and a circumference of $10\pi$ centimeters. What is the surface area of the cylinder?

**b.** What is the volume of the cylinder?

**5.** Find the volume of each of the following:

**a.** a sphere with a radius of 4 centimeters

**b.** a cone with a height of 10 inches and a base of radius 3 inches

**c.** a cylinder with a base area of $10\pi$ square centimeters and a height of 25 centimeters

## Additional Practice (continued)

**6.** Find the volume of each of the following:

**a.** a sphere with a diameter of 100 centimeters

**b.** a cylinder with a radius of 14 inches and a height of 1.5 feet

**c.** a cone with a base area of 11.5π square centimeters and a height of 20 centimeters

**7.** Find the volume of each figure. Round to the nearest 0.1 cubic centimeter.

**a.**

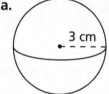

3 cm

**b.**

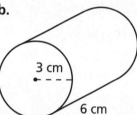

3 cm

6 cm

**c.**

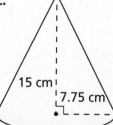

15 cm

7.75 cm

**d.**

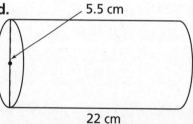

5.5 cm

22 cm

Name _____ Date _____ Class _____

## Additional Practice (continued)

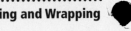

**8.** The two cones below are similar.

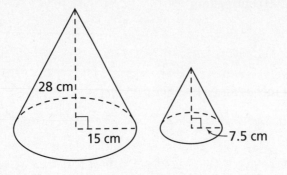

**a.** What is the height of the smaller cone?

**b.** What is the volume of the larger cone?

**c.** What is the volume of the smaller cone?

**d.** Angie is using the smaller cone to scoop popcorn into the larger cone. How many scoops from the smaller cone will it take to fill the larger cone?

# Additional Practice *(continued)*

**9.** A sphere has a diameter of 4 meters. What is its volume?

**10. a.** Find the volume of this cylinder:

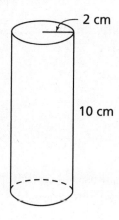

2 cm

10 cm

**b.** What is the volume if the height is doubled?

**c.** What is the volume if the radius of the base is doubled?

**d.** What is the volume if both the height and the radius of the base are doubled?

## **Additional Practice** (continued)

**11.** A cone has a height of 12 centimeters and a base with a radius of 4 centimeters.

    **a.** The cone is scaled down to a similar cone with one-eighth of the original volume. What are the dimensions of the scaled-down cone?

    **b.** Is your answer to part (a) the only possibility for the dimensions of the scaled-down cone? Explain your reasoning.

**12. a.** How does the volume of a sphere with a radius of 4 centimeters compare to the volume of a sphere with a radius of 6 centimeters? Explain your reasoning.

    **b.** Are the 4-centimeter sphere and the 6-centimeter sphere similar? Explain your reasoning.

**13.** When a ball is immersed in water, it displaces $36\pi$ cubic centimeters of water. What is the radius of the ball?

# Additional Practice (continued)

14. A conical cup is partially filled with water as shown in the diagram below. Use the diagram to answer the following questions.

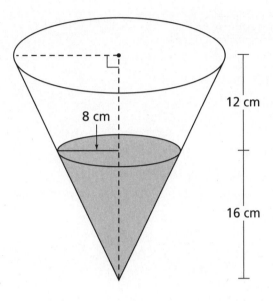

a. What is the radius of the top of the cup? Explain your reasoning.

b. What is the volume of the water in the cup?

c. What is the volume of the cup? Explain.

15. When a cube is dropped into a cylinder partially filled with water, 125 milliliters of water are displaced. What is the length of each edge of the cube? Explain your reasoning.

Name _____ Date _____ Class _____

# Additional Practice *(continued)*

**16. a.** Complete the table below for each rectangular box. A 1-2-3 box means a box with dimensions $1 \times 2 \times 3$.

| Closed Box | Surface Area | Volume |
|---|---|---|
| A: 1-2-3 box | | |
| B: 2-4-6 box | | |
| C: 3-6-9 box | | |
| D: 4-8-12 box | | |

**b.** Use your table from part (a) to complete the table below.

| Compare the Boxes | Scale Factor | Change in Surface Area | Change in Volume |
|---|---|---|---|
| From A to B | | | |
| From A to C | | | |
| From A to D | | | |
| From B to C | | | |
| From B to D | | | |
| From C to D | | | |

# Additional Practice: Digital Assessments

**17.** Draw a line to connect each net with the three-dimensional figure that can be formed from it.

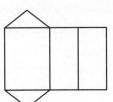

cone

cylinder

hexagonal prism

hexagonal pyramid

triangular prism

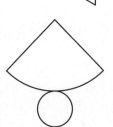

triangular pyramid

**18.** A cylindrical piston on an industrial engine has a radius of 2 meters and a height of 4 meters. Circle the answers that correctly complete each statement. The surface area of the piston is

$$\begin{bmatrix} A = 2\pi(2)^2 + 2\pi(2) \\ A = 2\pi(2)^2 + 2\pi(2)(4) \\ A = \pi(2)^2 + \pi(2)(4) \\ A = \pi(2)^2 + 2\pi(2)(4) \end{bmatrix}, \text{ which is}$$

approximately $\begin{bmatrix} 37.68 \\ 75.36 \\ 31.40 \\ 62.80 \end{bmatrix}$ square meters.

The volume of the piston is

$$\begin{bmatrix} V = \pi(2)^2(4) \\ V = \pi(4)^2(2) \\ V = \pi(2)(4) \end{bmatrix}, \text{ which}$$

simplifies to approximately $\begin{bmatrix} 50.24 \\ 100.48 \\ 25.12 \\ 12.56 \end{bmatrix}$ cubic meters.

**19.** Write the letters of the figures in order from least to greatest volume.

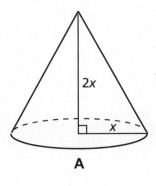

A

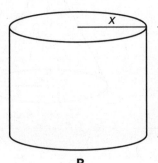

B

C

☐ , ☐ , ☐

# Skill: Volume of a Cylinder, Cone, or Sphere

**Name each three-dimensional figure.**

1.

2.

3.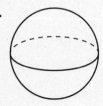

4.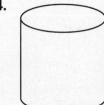

**Find the volume of each cone or cylinder. Round your answer to the nearest cubic unit.**

5.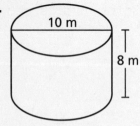

6.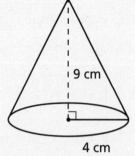

Name _____ Date _____ Class _____

# Skill: Volume of a Cylinder, Cone, or Sphere (continued)

For Exercises 7–10, find the volume of each cylinder, cone, or sphere. Round your answer to the nearest cubic unit.

**7.**
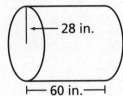
28 in.
60 in.

**8.**
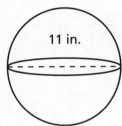
11 in.

**9.**
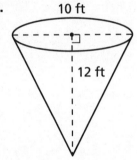
10 ft
12 ft

**10.**
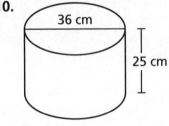
36 cm
25 cm

**11.** A water storage tank has a cylindrical shape. The base has a diameter of 18 meters, and the tank is 32 meters high. How much water, to the nearest cubic unit, can the tank hold?

**12.** A cylindrical juice container is 9 inches tall and has a radius of 2 inches. What is the volume of the container to the nearest whole unit?

Name _____ Date _____ Class _____

# Skill: Nets and Surface Area

Name the three-dimensional shape you can form from each net.

1.

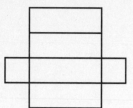

2.

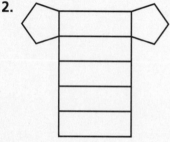

3.

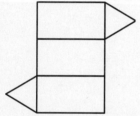

4.

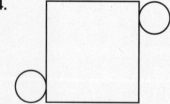

# Skill: Nets and Surface Area (continued)

**Find the surface area of each figure to the nearest square unit.**

**5.**  53 cm

102 cm

**6.**  28 in.

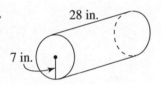

7 in.

**7.**  $d$ = 44 ft

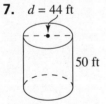

50 ft

# Skill: Cones, Pyramids, and Spheres

**Find the volume of each figure to the nearest cubic unit.**

1.
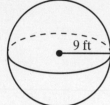
9 ft

2.
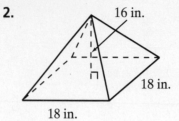
16 in.
18 in.
18 in.

3.
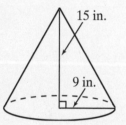
15 in.
9 in.

4.
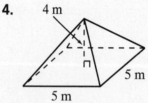
4 m
5 m
5 m

5.
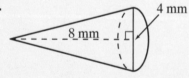
4 mm
8 mm

6.
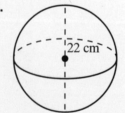
22 cm

# Additional Practice

Below are two bar graphs showing data about Leah and Elia's reaction times.

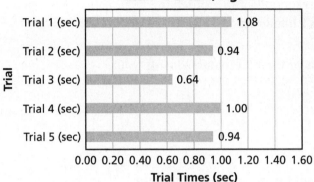

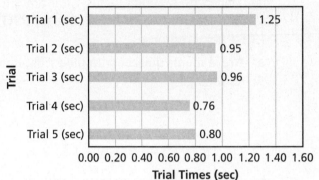

1. Determine the following statistics for each student.

   a. mean

   b. median

   c. spread

   d. range

   e. mean absolute deviation

2. Compare Elia's reaction times to Leah's reaction times.

   a. Is one student quicker than the other student? Explain your reasoning.

   b. Is one student more consistent than the other student? Explain.

# Additional Practice (continued)

3. The sample of data below is from 25 female students and 25 male students. In an experiment students responded to a stimulus, once with their right hands and once with their left hands. Their times to respond were recorded in seconds. Below are two graphs, one for RIGHT hand responses and one for LEFT hand responses.

   a. Are students quicker with their right hands or their left hands? Justify your reasoning.

   b. Are students more consistent with their right hands or their left hands? Justify your reasoning.

   c. Some of the students may have been left handed. Which students do you think these were? Justify your reasoning.

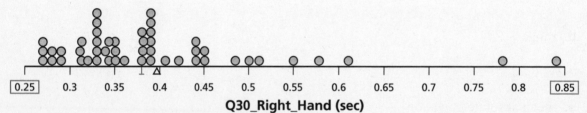

**Q30_Right_Hand (sec)**

The mean is 0.39702 sec and the median is 0.38 sec.

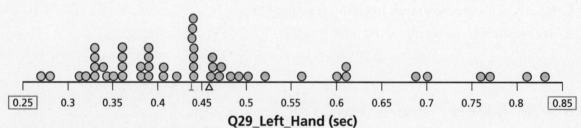

**Q29_Left_Hand (sec)**

The mean is 0.45726 sec and the median is 0.4375 sec.

SOURCE: www.censusonline.net

# Additional Practice *(continued)*

4. Using the same data set about reaction times, compare the male reaction times with their right hands to the female reaction times with their right hands. Look at the graphs below.

Male

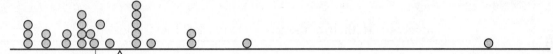

Female

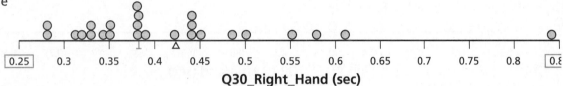

**Q30_Right_Hand (sec)**

Males: mean = 0.37124 sec and median = 0.344 sec
Females: mean = 0.4228 sec and median = 0.382 sec

  a. For females and males, the means and medians are different. What accounts for this happening?

  b. Identify the range and interquartile range (IQR) of each distribution.

  c. Are females quicker than males using their right hands? Justify your reasoning.

  d. Are females more consistent than males using their right hands? Justify your reasoning.

# Additional Practice *(continued)*

**5.** Using the same data set about reaction times, compare the male reaction times with their left hands to the female reaction times with their left hands. Look at the graphs below.

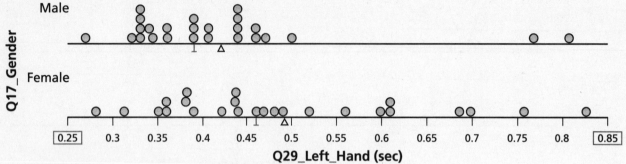

Males: mean = 0.42128 sec and median = 0.39 sec
Females: mean = 0.49324 sec and median = 0.461 sec

**a.** For females and males, the means and medians are different. What might account for this happening?

**b.** Are females quicker than males using their left hands? Justify your reasoning.

**c.** Are females more consistent than males using their left hands? Justify your reasoning.

# Additional Practice *(continued)*

**6.** Are wood coasters longer than steel coasters? Use the roller coaster graphs below to help answer the question.

Use these strategies and others that make sense to you:

**a.** Compare statistics (ranges, medians, means) for the two types of roller coasters.

**b.** Partition the distributions at benchmark lengths and look at the percents of each type of roller coaster at and above or below this speed. For example, for *length* you could look at the percent of wood and percent of steel roller coasters with lengths at and above or below 1,000 feet, 2,000 feet, 3,000 feet, 4,000 feet, and so on.

### Steel Coasters

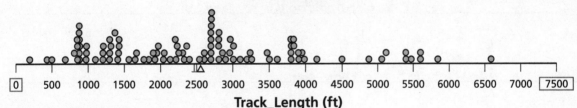

**Track_Length (ft)**

Mean = 2548, median = 2468.5, spread = 198–6595

### Wood Coasters

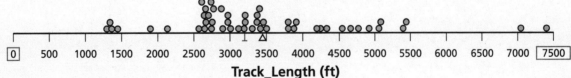

**Track_Length (ft)**

Mean = 3450.78, median = 3200, spread = 1800–7400

# Additional Practice (continued)

**7.** Look at the graph showing track length and duration of rides for 150 roller
coasters. Write three observations about the relationship between track length
and duration of ride.

**Roller Coasters: Track Length and Duration of Ride**

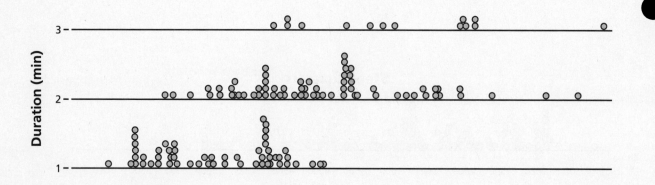

## Additional Practice *(continued)*

**8.** Edwin was playing a game but wondered if the two number cubes he was
using were fair. He rolled the suspicious number cubes 36 times and found
the sum of the two numbers on the top faces. Then he compared the results
to 100 rolls of two fair number cubes that had been completed in his
mathematics class.

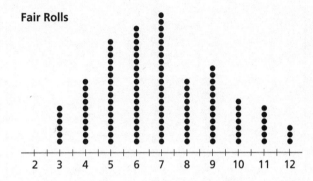

**a.** Write three statements comparing the distribution of sums for the two sets
of number cubes.

**b.** Find the mean and mean absolute deviation (MAD) for each set of sums.

**c.** For each data set of rolls, determine how many values are located within
one MAD and write this number as a percent of the total rolls.

**d.** Do you think the suspicious number cubes are fair? Explain your answer.

# Additional Practice: Digital Assessments

**9.** Maxine rolled a number cube 100 times and graphed the outcomes. What is true regarding her data? *Select all that apply.*

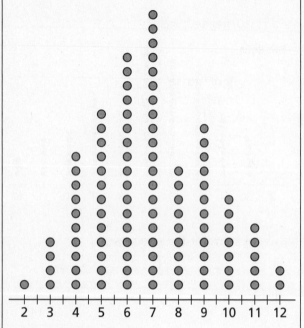

- ☐ The mean is 6.9.
- ☐ The mean is 7.0.
- ☐ The median is 6.9.
- ☐ The median is 7.0.
- ☐ The range is 12.
- ☐ The mean absolute deviation is 1.79.
- ☐ The spread is from 0 to 12.

**10.** Below is a bar graph showing Sammy's reaction times on several trials. Use the tiles to fill in each box for an equation that calculates her mean reaction time.

**Sammy's Reaction Times**

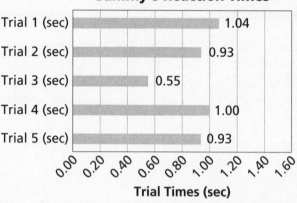

Trial 1 (sec)  1.04
Trial 2 (sec)  0.93
Trial 3 (sec)  0.55
Trial 4 (sec)  1.00
Trial 5 (sec)  0.93

0.00  0.20  0.40  0.60  0.80  1.00  1.20  1.40  1.60

**Trial Times (sec)**

| 5 | 4 | 1.04 | 0.93 |
| 0.89 | 1.00 | 0.55 | 0.88 |

$$\frac{\boxed{\phantom{0}} + \boxed{\phantom{0}} + \boxed{\phantom{0}} + \boxed{\phantom{0}} + \boxed{\phantom{0}}}{\boxed{\phantom{0}}} = \boxed{\phantom{0}}$$

**11.** The dot plots represent the scores on the last two tests taken by Mrs. Roberto's math students. Circle the words and numbers that make the statements true.

The test scores on $\begin{bmatrix} \text{Test 1} \\ \text{Test 2} \end{bmatrix}$ had the greater range.

The test scores on $\begin{bmatrix} \text{Test 1} \\ \text{Test 2} \end{bmatrix}$ had the greater mean.

The test scores on $\begin{bmatrix} \text{Test 1} \\ \text{Test 2} \end{bmatrix}$ had the greater MAD.

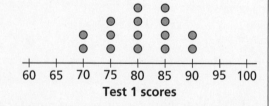

60  65  70  75  80  85  90  95  100

**Test 1 scores**

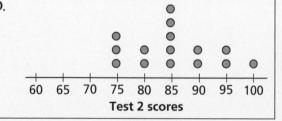

60  65  70  75  80  85  90  95  100

**Test 2 scores**

# Additional Practice

**For Exercises 1–2,**

    **a.** Describe the *population*, *sampling plan*, and *sample*.

    **b.** Identify the type of sampling plan that is used. Explain if the sampling plan will result in a representative sample.

    **c.** Recommend any changes to the sampling plan that are needed. Justify your recommendation.

**1.** The manager of a movie theater wants to know which types of movies are preferred by teenagers and young adults in the town. The movie house shows movies from 1 P.M. to 10 P.M. An employee records the age of every movie-goer who purchases a ticket from 7 P.M. to 8 P.M.

**2.** A school newspaper wants to write an article about activities to do on school holidays. They write the names of the 24 homeroom teachers on cards, and then choose 4 cards. The students in these 4 classes are given surveys about what they do on several school holidays.

# Additional Practice (continued)

For Exercises 3–4,

    a. Describe the *population*, *sampling plan*, and *sample*.

    b. Identify the type of sampling plan that is used. Explain if the sampling plan will result in a representative sample.

    c. Recommend any changes to the sampling plan that are needed. Justify your recommendation.

**3.** A pizza restaurant wants to know which crust is the favorite of its customers. It records the crust type of every fifth pizza purchased for one day.

**4.** The manager of a news magazine wants to know how much time people of different ages spend on digital media to communicate with friends. The magazine posts a link to a survey on their website and asks readers to click the link and submit their responses.

Name _____ Date _____ Class _____

## Additional Practice (continued)

**For Exercises 5–6,**

   **a.** Describe the *population*, *sampling plan*, and *sample*.

   **b.** Identify the type of sampling plan that is used. Explain if the sampling plan will result in a representative sample.

   **c.** Recommend any changes to the sampling plan that are needed. Justify your recommendation.

**5.** A school administration wants to know what educational topics the teachers would like to learn more about, and how they would like to learn about these topics. The administration sends an email to every teacher with a link to the survey.

**6.** A testing company uses a computer to score 5,000 tests. To check for accurate scoring, the computer is programmed to randomly choose 250 tests for scoring by 3 employees.

# Additional Practice (continued)

**Use the following information for Exercises 7–9.**

A math class wants to study the effects of cell phones as distractions to learning. They design an experiment with a 10 question multiple-choice test to be given after watching a 30-minute video where cell phone usage is allowed. Along with the test, participants will be asked to estimate the number of times they looked at their phones and how many minutes total they spent looking at the phones.

The video is shown to 300 students at the school during an assembly. The students all take the test and cell phone use survey in their classrooms right after the assembly. The results are given to the math class, ordered by number of questions answered correctly on the test.

7. Ana suggests randomly choosing 10 test results to create a sample distribution. Raquel suggests choosing every tenth test result from the list. Whose sample could be used to draw conclusions about the effects of cell phone usage on learning? Explain.

8. Three students each use a random number generator to choose 50 test results to create sampling distributions of the test scores. How would you expect the distributions to be similar? How would you expect the distributions to differ? Explain.

9. Another three students analyze the results of the cell phone survey to compare the total number of times a participant looked a cell phone. Alison created a line plot for the first 50 results from the list. Tony created a line plot for 30 results randomly chosen using a random number generator. Harmon created a line plot for using every fifth result from the list.

   Which student's line plot would you expect to be the most similar to a line plot of the population's cell phone use? The least similar? Explain your reasoning.

# Additional Practice: Digital Assessments

**10.** An office manager wants to know what type of cake he should serve at next month's meeting. He sends an email to every office worker with a link to the survey. Which statements are true? *Select all that apply.*

☐ The population is the office manager.

☐ The population is every office worker.

☐ The sampling plan is serving cake at next month's meeting.

☐ The sampling plan is sending an email to every office worker.

☐ The sample is the office manager.

☐ The sample is every office worker.

**11.** Circle the words or phrases that best complete the statements.

A researcher wants to estimate the growth in a colony of 300 mice. She can do this by choosing 10 random mice

to create a ⎡ mean
⎢ sample
⎢ sample distribution
⎣ survey ⎤ .

The random mice can be drawn from the colony by making a list with all the mice

by age and ⎡ choosing every 10th mouse
⎢ choosing the last 10 mice
⎢ choosing every 30th mouse
⎣ choosing the first 30 mice ⎤ .

This sampling method would be as valid

as ⎡ using a random number generator
⎢ choosing her favorite mice
⎢ looking for the largest mice
⎣ rolling a six-sided number cube ⎤ .

**12.** The line plot shows the time in seconds of 15 racers in a sprint. Shade the circles below the line plot that mark the mean and median scores.

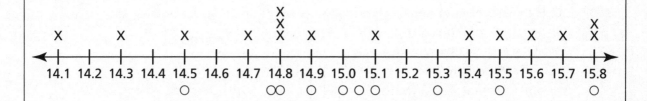

# Skill: Sample Distributions

The table of data shows the weights, in pounds, of babies born at a hospital over a one-week period.

| Baby | 01 | 02 | 03 | 04 | 05 | 06 | 07 | 08 | 09 | 10 |
|---|---|---|---|---|---|---|---|---|---|---|
| Weight (lbs) | 7.5 | 7.1 | 8.0 | 7.7 | 6.8 | 8.5 | 8.6 | 8.3 | 7.5 | 8.9 |
| Baby | 11 | 12 | 13 | 14 | 15 | 16 | 17 | 18 | 19 | 20 |
| Weight (lbs) | 8.8 | 9.0 | 8.8 | 6.9 | 7.1 | 7.2 | 5.8 | 7.2 | 9.0 | 7.4 |
| Baby | 21 | 22 | 23 | 24 | 25 | 26 | 27 | 28 | 29 | 30 |
| Weight (lbs) | 6.6 | 7.2 | 8.6 | 7.6 | 8.2 | 6.4 | 9.1 | 7.1 | 7.6 | 5.8 |
| Baby | 31 | 32 | 33 | 34 | 35 | 36 | 37 | 38 | 39 | 40 |
| Weight (lbs) | 8.1 | 7.4 | 7.1 | 8.4 | 7.6 | 8.0 | 8.1 | 6.9 | 8.6 | 6.9 |
| Baby | 41 | 42 | 43 | 44 | 45 | 46 | 47 | 48 | 49 | 50 |
| Weight (lbs) | 5.4 | 8.9 | 9.7 | 6.9 | 7.6 | 9.1 | 7.2 | 6.8 | 6.4 | 8.9 |

Find the mean and median weights for each sample of 10 babies.

1. Babies 01–10

2. Babies 11–20

3. Babies 21–30

4. Babies 31–40

5. Babies 41–50

# Skill: Sample Distributions (continued)

The table of data shows the weights, in pounds, of babies born at a hospital over a one-week period.

| Baby | 01 | 02 | 03 | 04 | 05 | 06 | 07 | 08 | 09 | 10 |
|---|---|---|---|---|---|---|---|---|---|---|
| Weight (lbs) | 7.5 | 7.1 | 8.0 | 7.7 | 6.8 | 8.5 | 8.6 | 8.3 | 7.5 | 8.9 |
| Baby | 11 | 12 | 13 | 14 | 15 | 16 | 17 | 18 | 19 | 20 |
| Weight (lbs) | 8.8 | 9.0 | 8.8 | 6.9 | 7.1 | 7.2 | 5.8 | 7.2 | 9.0 | 7.4 |
| Baby | 21 | 22 | 23 | 24 | 25 | 26 | 27 | 28 | 29 | 30 |
| Weight (lbs) | 6.6 | 7.2 | 8.6 | 7.6 | 8.2 | 6.4 | 9.1 | 7.1 | 7.6 | 5.8 |
| Baby | 31 | 32 | 33 | 34 | 35 | 36 | 37 | 38 | 39 | 40 |
| Weight (lbs) | 8.1 | 7.4 | 7.1 | 8.4 | 7.6 | 8.0 | 8.1 | 6.9 | 8.6 | 6.9 |
| Baby | 41 | 42 | 43 | 44 | 45 | 46 | 47 | 48 | 49 | 50 |
| Weight (lbs) | 5.4 | 8.9 | 9.7 | 6.9 | 7.6 | 9.1 | 7.2 | 6.8 | 6.4 | 8.9 |

Find the mean and median weights for each sample of 10 babies.

**6.** Every 5th baby

**7.** Babies 01, 02, 13, 14, 25, 26, 37, 38, 49, 50

**8.** Babies 03, 04, 10, 16, 19, 25, 31, 33, 40, 42

**9.** Babies 02, 08, 12, 18, 22, 28, 32, 38, 42, 48

**10.** Babies 07, 09, 13, 16, 17, 21, 25, 29, 36, 45

# Skill: Sample Distributions *(continued)*

**The mean weight of the babies is 7.7 pounds and the median weight of the babies is 7.6 pounds.**

**11.** Create a dot plot representing the means from Exercises 1–10. Mark the population mean with an X.

**12.** Create a dot plot representing the medians from Exercises 1–10. Mark the population median with an X.

**13.** How close were the sample means and medians to the population mean and median?

# Additional Practice

1. Carla and Diego are comparing the characteristics of two musical genres. One feature that they compare is the length in minutes of top songs in each genre. They use a list of the top 30 songs from the country and rock listing in an online store to create the following two box plots to compare song lengths.

**Top Country Song Length (min)**

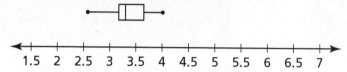

**Top Rock Song Length (min)**

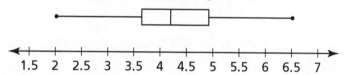

Carla and Diego wonder if similar results would occur using a different online store for music. They created the box plot but forgot to title it.

**Mystery Song Length (min)**

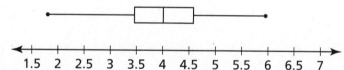

What genre of songs is likely represented by the mystery distribution of song lengths? Explain your reasoning.

# Additional Practice (continued)

Use the information below for Exercises 2–5.

A sports journalist is analyzing the records of a local golf team. She makes a table to display the points earned at eight 3-game tournaments by two golfers.

| A. Smith's Tournament Scores | | |
|---|---|---|
| Game 1 | Game 2 | Game 3 |
| 81 | 81 | 83 |
| 83 | 72 | 80 |
| 82 | 84 | 80 |
| 74 | 80 | 81 |
| 80 | 83 | 79 |
| 78 | 90 | 78 |
| 80 | 72 | 80 |
| 82 | 76 | 76 |

| S. Johnson's Tournament Scores | | |
|---|---|---|
| Game 1 | Game 2 | Game 3 |
| 76 | 77 | 79 |
| 76 | 76 | 76 |
| 83 | 82 | 82 |
| 78 | 79 | 75 |
| 77 | 71 | 78 |
| 77 | 80 | 75 |
| 83 | 77 | 77 |
| 80 | 76 | 75 |

**2. a.** Make a line plot displaying all the tournament scores of A. Smith. Make another line plot displaying all the tournament scores of S. Johnson.

**b.** What is the mean of each set of data? The MAD?

**c.** On each line plot, mark the locations of one MAD and two MADs less than and greater than the mean.

**3.** Is the mean score of A. Smith an unexpected data value on the line plot for S. Johnson's scores? Explain.

**4.** Is the mean score of S. Johnson an unexpected data value on the line plot for A. Smith's scores? Explain.

# Additional Practice (continued)

Use the information below for Exercises 5–7.

Quentin works in a college cafeteria. He opens a box containing 80 cups of cereal with raisins. He selects a sample of 20 cups of cereal and counts the raisins in each cup. The table shows Quentin's data.

| Cup Number | Number of Raisins | | Cup Number | Number of Raisins |
|---|---|---|---|---|
| 1 | 8 | | 11 | 13 |
| 2 | 11 | | 12 | 15 |
| 3 | 7 | | 13 | 11 |
| 4 | 8 | | 14 | 10 |
| 5 | 9 | | 15 | 12 |
| 6 | 10 | | 16 | 10 |
| 7 | 12 | | 17 | 9 |
| 8 | 14 | | 18 | 14 |
| 9 | 10 | | 19 | 12 |
| 10 | 9 | | 20 | 12 |

5. Estimate the total number of raisins in the box. Explain your answer.

6. Complete each statement with the most appropriate fraction: $\frac{1}{4}$, $\frac{1}{2}$, or $\frac{2}{3}$.

   a. More than _____ of the 1-cup servings of cereal have at least 10 raisins.

   b. About _____ of the 1-cup servings of cereal have at least 11 raisins.

   c. More than _____ of the 1-cup servings of cereal have at least 12 raisins.

7. a. The cereal has an advertising slogan "At least 10 raisins in every single serving!" Do you think this is an accurate slogan? Explain.

   b. Suggest a new advertising slogan.

# Additional Practice (continued)

**8.** Kyra wants to estimate the number of pennies in a jar. She removes 50 pennies and marks them with a yellow dot. Then she returns the pennies to the jar and mixes them with the unmarked pennies. She takes 5 samples from the jar. The table shows her data.

| Sample | Total Number of Pennies | Number of Pennies with Yellow Dot | Relative Frequency |
|--------|--------|--------|--------|
| 1 | 20 | 4 | |
| 2 | 38 | 3 | |
| 3 | 52 | 5 | |
| 4 | 77 | 8 | |
| 5 | 41 | 4 | |

**a.** Fill out the last column of the table with the relative frequency of the total pennies that are marked with yellow dots for each sample.

**b.** Which sample has the greatest precent of marked pennies? The least percent? Use these samples to find two estimates for the number of pennies in the jar. Show your work.

**c.** A sample of 100 pennies is pulled from the jar. How many pennies would you expect to be marked with yellow dots? Explain your reasoning.

**d.** Estimate the number of pennies in the jar. Explain your reasoning.

# Additional Practice: Digital Assessments

**9.** The box plot below shows the height of pea plants in inches. Which of the following statements are true? *Select all that apply.*

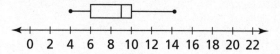

0  2  4  6  8  10  12  14  16  18  20  22

☐ The median is 10.

☐ The median is 8.

☐ The median is 9.

☐ The interquartile range is 12.

☐ The interquartile range is 4.

☐ The interquartile range is 8.

☐ The range is 5.

☐ The range is 15.

☐ The range is 10.

**10.** Tyson wants to estimate how many marbles are in a bag. He marks 10 marbles and returns them to the bag. He takes three samples from the bag, with the following data:

| Sample | Total number of marbles | Number of marked marbles |
|--------|-------------------------|--------------------------|
| 1 | 33 | 3 |
| 2 | 21 | 2 |
| 3 | 18 | 2 |

The ratio of marked marbles drawn each time ranged from about $\begin{bmatrix} 0.09 \\ 0.9 \\ 0.11 \\ 0.01 \end{bmatrix}$ to about

0.11. Since approximately $\begin{bmatrix} 1\% \\ 10\% \\ 20\% \\ 30\% \end{bmatrix}$ of each

sample is marked marbles, there are

approximately $\begin{bmatrix} 100 \\ 1{,}000 \\ 200 \end{bmatrix}$ marbles in the bag.

**11.** The chart below shows Jason's scores from 10 dart games he played Friday night. Which box plot shows this data?

| Game 1 | 350 |
|--------|-----|
| Game 2 | 455 |
| Game 3 | 432 |
| Game 4 | 368 |
| Game 5 | 359 |
| Game 6 | 421 |
| Game 7 | 399 |
| Game 8 | 409 |
| Game 9 | 428 |
| Game 10 | 398 |

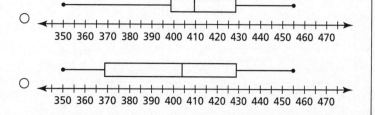

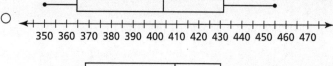

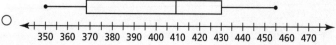

# Skill: Box Plots

Identify the median, range, and interquartile range for each box plot.

**1.**

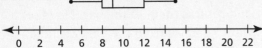

**2.**

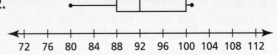

**3.**

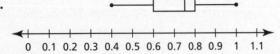

**4.**

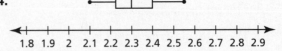

**5.**

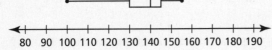

**6.**

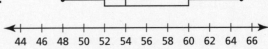

**7.**

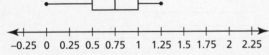

**8.**

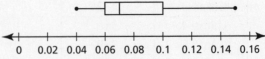

# Skill: Box Plots (continued)

**Represent each set of data with a box plot.**

**9.** 32, 33, 36, 40, 31, 28, 33, 40

**10.** 200, 220, 200, 180, 180, 200, 250, 210

**11.** 1.4, 1.1, 1.2, 1.4, 0.7, 1.2, 1.8, 1.2, 1.0, 1.0

**12.** 4, 4, 4, 7, 2, 5, 4, 7, 8, 9, 5, 6, 3, 5

**13.** 36, 30, 28, 22, 25, 19, 26, 24, 24, 27